Whips of Westfield

The Rise and Decline of an American Industry

Westfield, Massachusetts

Bruce W. Cortis

Copyright © 2018 Bruce W. Cortis

Off the Common Books
Amherst, Massachusetts

www.levellerspress.com/off-the-common-books

All rights reserved including the right of
reproduction in whole or in part in any form.

Printed in the United States of America

ISBN 978-1-945473-76-0

Dedication

This book is dedicated to my wife, Carolyn J. Cortis, who for the last 46 years of our marriage, has continually supported my career and research efforts, while also raising our three children, Tim, B.J. and Kelly.

Without her continual support and encouragement, this book likely would never have been completed.

Bruce W. Cortis

Acknowledgements

I would like to acknowledge and thank the following people for their assistance and contributions to my research, without their contributions completion of this book would not have been possible.

Ralph E. Cortis, Dr. Robert Brown, Kate Deviny, Joyce Peregrin, Tommy Stanziola, Chris Erickson, Joe Sibley, Dennis Picard and Bradlee Gage of Amherst, Ma.

Special thanks to my family and extended family for their support and encouragement throughout the last two years which kept me going.

Also, Kathy Arnold and Carolyn Cortis for assisting with proof-reading the book and providing suggestions to my writing.

Additional thanks to the Westfield Athenaeum for the research assistance and their gracious sharing of many of the images throughout the book. The Athenaeum's archives contain a wealth of information pertaining to Westfield's history and I highly encourage the public to support their activities and make use of their resources.

Front Cover: American Whip Company Factory, 1865
               Courtesy Westfield Athenaeum, Westfield, Ma.

Back Cover: Assorted Whip Labels
               Courtesy Tommy Stanziola, Westfield, Ma.

Table of Contents

Foreword 1

Introduction 3

Whip Construction and Materials 5

Specialty Whips 11

Labor 15

Fires & Floods 21

Patents 29

Early Era (1810-1855)..39

    The Whip Plaiting/Braiding Machine – Who was first ? 45

    Early Whip Manufacturers - 1825-55.. 47

Middle Era (1855 - 1893)

    Whips become a dominant industry 57

    American Whip Company, establishment of a dynasty 65

    The 'Combination' 83

    The Whip 'Syndicate' - beginning of the consolidation............ 91

Modern Era (1893 – Present)

    United States Whip Corporation formed, Dec. 29, 1892.......... 97

    The Whip's final chapter as a major Westfield Industry......... 105

    Westfield's Whip District 109

Westfield's Whip Industry in Pictures 113

Whip Company Profiles

    American Whip Company, est. 1855 141

    United States Whip Company, est. 12/29/1892 145

    Chronological listing of Companies 149

Summary 203

Appendixes 205

    John Thorpe Patent Application Letter, 1821 207

    Westfield Whip Manufacturers – Sorted by Name 209

    Westfield Whip Patents Sorted by Year and Number 219

    Westfield Whip Patents Sorted by Name 231

Bibliography 241

Foreword

Often when a person undertakes researching a topic for a book, there's an underlying event or deeper connection which was the impetus for taking on the effort.

Having grown up in Westfield in the 1960's, the city's nickname of 'Whip City' was ingrained in our daily lives. However, more recently I have observed how the public's awareness of the history of the whip industry and how important it was to Westfield's development in the 19th century has been gradually fading.

With this compilation, I have attempted to present a framework of the history of Westfield's whip industry. By no means is this a complete history of all of the events, companies or individuals who contributed to Westfield becoming the "Whip City of the World".

My goal with this book is to establish a source which will; first, educate people who are not aware of Westfield's whip heritage and second, provide information to assist those who want to dig deeper into researching particular companies or areas by establishing reference points to assist their efforts.

While I have tried my best to be as accurate as possible, there are apt to be omissions and hopefully, just a few minor errors.

Hopefully, this compilation of data will enhance an overall understanding of the evolution of Westfield's whip industry, the impact on Westfield's economy, the involvement of its people and its ultimate demise.

Introduction

Much has been written regarding the whip industry of Westfield, Massachusetts in newspapers, historical accounts, various publications, and individual papers during the last 100 years. However, while many of those accounts have described the most well-known whip makers and companies, there is a significant amount of additional information regarding the evolution of the industry and the men associated with the industry that hasn't been compiled in a single volume.

Westfield whip manufacturers also had strong linkages and interactions with whip companies in many states across the United States. The involvement of the Westfield manufacturers in conjunction with those external companies in controlling the whip industry hasn't previously been included in discussions about Westfield's whip industry.

As with any research project of this nature, data collection and verification of that data becomes more and more difficult the further back in time you research. The whip industry is no exception to this dilemma. From the early 1800's until approximately 1850, first hand records are very sparse. Historical and biographical accounts, sometimes compiled decades after the actual events, are prone to inaccuracies or omitted data.

Another challenge with being able to document when companies were started and their length of their existence was the frequency of name changes. Often a company would exist for just a year or two before ceasing to exist or merging with a partner resulting in a name change. On occasion, after partnership were dissolved, with each partner resumed operations under their old names. However, more often one or both of the partners would establish relationships with new partners resulting in additional variations of company names. This pattern of name changes was frequent throughout the remainder of the nineteenth century. As the century wore on, acquisitions of the smaller shops by the larger firms became more frequent and old company names would sometimes simply fade from existence. However, in many cases companies which had been acquired by the larger firms continued to be advertised under their own labels as though they were still in operation, adding to the difficulty in establishing when they ceased truly manufacturing whips in their own factories.

The information contained in this compilation was derived from a wide set of resources. Early newspaper accounts provided valuable information to some of the larger firms and public events. However, they offered limited information for the smaller companies or individual contributors. A wide range of local, state and federal documents, Westfield city directories, obituaries, maps and atlases were used to compile the information about Westfield's whip industry, its men and their companies.

However, virtually every source of information encountered during this research has been proven to be incomplete or containing errors ranging from minor to significant in nature, necessitating the need to correlate those facts with other records from the same period.

Acknowledging that it is impossible to document every person or company who made significant contributions, I have tried to use all of the varied sources to compile as much information as possible.

As with any chronology of this nature there are several topics, while interleaved with the ongoing history, stand on their own, meriting their own specific discussion. These include: Whip Construction and Materials, Patents, Labor, Fires & Floods and Specialty Whips. These topics have been summarized before delving into the chronological history of the industry.

Whip Construction and Materials

It is not the intent of this book to concentrate on the techniques and processes of manufacturing whips, which could fill a book of its own. However, no work covering Westfield's whip industry would be complete without at least an overview of the evolution of whip construction.

In its simplest form, beginning in the early 1800's a whip was often little more than a piece of wood with a rawhide lash attached to the end of it. With the advent of more complex whips, additional materials were required and whip construction became increasingly complex.

Advertisement
Springfield Republican, Sprngfield, Ma.

The basic components of a whip are its stock or handle, a lash/thong and finally a snap attached to the end of the lash. With the introduction of braided stocks varying grades of thread of either cotton or silk were used for braiding the whips outer covering depending upon the level of quality of whip being made or its intended use.

Initially, the core of a whip was wood but it was soon replaced with whalebone as the material of choice for the stock of a braided whip. The whalebone used was actually the flexible baleen from the inside of a whale's mouth. The baleen was carefully cut and shaped. After a period of time, rattan was introduced to supplement the whalebone core to make a larger butt or stock while retaining the flexibility required. Strips of specially cut and shaped pieces of rattan or leather were wrapped around the core, glued and wrapped with rope. Once dry, the stock was turned on lathes and rolled to balance it.

Although various types of hide were used, Water buffalo was the preferred choice for the rawhide covering the stock. Like the whalebone and rattan, the rawhide required special cutting and treating before being braided to the stock. Over time whalebone became increasingly expensive and a wide variety of materials were attempted to be used to replace it, with varying degrees of success.

Once the handle/stock had been prepared, lashes of varying lengths with a snap at the end was attached to complete the whip. Caps or buttons of various types where added to the ends of the whip to finish the whip and keep the braiding from unraveling. Decorative rings (ferrules) where often added to the stocks as an embellishment. Expensive specialty whips manufactured for gifts or presentations often had ivory or gold decorative features added as embellishments. Engraving, fancy labels and a variety of other means to decorate the whips were also common.

The process of creating the whalebone core, gluing the rattan, shaping, rounding and balancing it, braiding the rawhide, attaching the lash & snap and finally braiding the outer covering was a manually intensive and complicated process involving many steps. These were all necessary to complete a perfectly round and balanced whip capable of performing to the highest standards. Even with the advent of machines in the early 1820-30's, many steps in the creation of a whip remained a manually intensive process.

The term 'plaiting' is widely used in discussing the manufacture of whips. The term is often used interchangeably with braiding. Plaiting (pronounced 'platting') is the process of weaving or braiding the outer covering of a whip. As such the material used (e.g. cotton, silk, etc.), the grade of thread, style of braiding and complexity of the braid all significantly affected the overall quality (and cost) of a whip.

The wide variety of materials used in the manufacture of whips can be seen in the following table from the *1889 Statistics of Manufacture for Massachusetts*. The table described the items to be included when calculating the value of stocks used in the manufacture of whips.

Whips, Lashes and Stocks	
Hides (whether cow or horse, and whether finished or raw)	*Lashes* (whether buckskin, horse-hide or other)
Leather (whether enameled or sole)	*Whips* (whether Rattan, rawhide, toy or other)
Lumber (whether oak, ash, basswood, beech, birch, hickory, maple, oak, rattan, walnut, or white-wood, and whether dressed or rough)	*Snaps* (whether cotton, linen or silk)
	Stocks (whether hickory, rattan or other)
Skins (whether buckskins, deerskins, goatskins, or sheepskins and whether dry, finished or slated)	*Other Articles* (All articles not previously specified)
Thread (whether cotton flax, hemp, jute, linen, mohair, or silk)	
Whalebone	

While Westfield became the center of the whip industry, it is significant to note that very little of the materials used in the construction of whips were native to the area. Whalebone was obtained from the whaling fleets of New England and other areas. Rawhide from water buffalo was imported from Asia. Rattan was imported from Indonesia and the Philippines. Initially, even the cotton thread for final braiding of the whip stock was brought in from other locales until Warren Threadworks was established in Westfield in 1880.

Beginning in the early 1800's and continuing through the nineteenth century, the construction of the whips, materials used and associated manufacturing processes were in a constant state of evolution as different companies competed with each other to gain or retain their market share.

The rising costs for materials such as whalebone and rattan drove manufacturers to experiment with a wide variety of materials and techniques to overcome those costs. Whip manufacturers promoted 'all leather' whips, whips of wound wire, twisted rawhide centers, different materials for coverings such as rubber, eel skin, sheep skin et al. The whip makers also used a variety of descriptions in an attempt to promote their whips as being equal or greater in quality to traditional whalebone core whips.

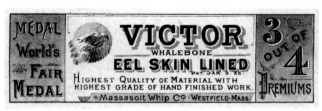

Courtesy Tommy Stanziola

Another method of reducing the use of whalebone was a half or three-quarter whalebone core used in an attempt to keep the original whalebone foundation while reducing the amount of the precious material for the whip.

One of the more innovative alternatives to whalebone was developed by E.K. Warren of Three Oaks, Michigan. In 1883, E. K. Warren invented a process for using cut up pieces of goose and turkey quills which were then glued together to create a material he patented under the name of 'Featherbone' as a whalebone replacement. Featherbone was successfully used in whips but it had even greater success as a whalebone replacement as a stiffener in women's corsets. The whip portion of E. K. Warren's Featherbone Co. eventually became part of the consolidation of whip companies in Westfield when it became associated with Independent Whip Co. in 1894.

Yet another attempt to market a replacement to whalebone was Horse Whip Co.'s label of 'ZebuAzo' in the early 1900's. According to a description in the *Town of Westfield, Mass Souvenir 1906*, ZeboAzo was described as follows:

> "The specialty is the ZebuAzo, made in all varieties, but of the highest grade. ZebuAzo is the bone and sinew of the animal kingdom, combined with vegetable and fiber. Rendering it a perfect substitute for whalebone in elasticity, but is far more durable."

At the same time whip construction and materials were evolving, a wide variety of machines and devices were invented and improved to keep pace with the competition. As will be seen in the discussion on whip patents, the number of whips patents related to machinery was heavily skewed in favor of the

Westfield manufacturers. From 1830 until 1900 almost 60% of the machine related whip patents were attributed to the Westfield firms.

Virtually every part of a whip experienced changes, improvements and customization. As the whips became more complex, specialization amongst the whip makers became more frequent. Multiple smaller firms specialized in making specific parts of the whip versus full whip construction. Several shops focused solely on making and turning handles/stocks, while others manufactured lashes, snaps, buttons, etc. In addition, braiding of lashes and snaps was often done by women in their own homes versus actually working in the factories.

Customization of the whips resulted in literally hundreds of models and styles of whips being manufactured by the larger companies. Handles and lashes could be ordered in a variety of lengths and different qualities involving a wide range of materials. The wide variety of decorative features, such as ferrules, buttons, engraving and other customized embellishments made for a virtually unlimited variety of whips available to the customer. However, the steps required to manufacture customized whips which were highly valued by many customers became an obstacle to improving efficiency as the need to reduce costs became critical to sustaining profitability.

With many of the materials used for whips being imported from other locations, it was only natural that local businesses were spawned to satisfy some of those needs. One of the early supporting businesses was creation of a glue factory to satisfy the needs for the large quantities used to make whips. A newspaper article titled 'The Whip Manufacture' which was printed in multiple newspapers in June of 1833 described the glue factory.

> "the establishment of a glue manufactory, where a considerable quantity has been made within two years; and experiments are now in progress for the manufacture of Prussian Blue from the refuse pieces of horn from the Whip factories."

Another example of an enterprise which was established in Westfield to satisfy the needs of the whip industry was the William Warren Thread Co. Prior to Warren Thread establishing its Westfield factory in 1881, all of the cotton and silk thread used for the braiding of whips had to be brought in from other locations. In addition to fulfilling the needs of the local factories, Warren Thread would expand its product line of high quality threads well beyond needs of the whip industry.

Warren Thread next established a partnership with Mr. John Foster who held patents on machines for winding cord and thread. The resulting Foster Machine Company's devices wound thread on bobbins, spools, cylinders and cones of all kinds. In addition to being used by the Warren Thread Co., Foster Machine's winding machines were used all over the world.

Foster Machine Co. would survive both the whip industry and Warren Thread as a major Westfield industrial employer. The company was sold to Whiting Machine Works in 1963 and moved to Whitinsville, Ma. in 1964.

Specialty Whips

Specialty whips were presented as gifts to prominent citizens and politicians on several occasions by the Westfield manufacturers. A few of the well-known and more publicized recipients of whips included: Henry Clay, Daniel Webster, Gen H.J. Kilpatrick and Presidents John Tyler, Ulysses S. Grant and Abraham Lincoln.

1833, Henry Clay, Orator, Senator (Ky)

One of the earliest gifts of a specially manufactured whip to a prominent public figure was the whip given to Henry Clay. The gift received wide coverage in newspapers across the nation. On Jun 17, 1833, The *Connecticut Courant* of Hartford Ct. describes the whip as follows:

> "At Mr. Day's factory, we saw the elegant whip which was made there, and intended as a present from the friends of domestic industry in Westfield, to Henry Clay. About one third of the stock is ivory, inlaid with gold, and inscribed to the illustrious statesman. The remainder of the stock is pure whalebone, and the lashes is nine feet long. It is said to have cost $50 and is fine workmanship throughout."

The same article was reposted on June 23 in the *Charleston Courier*, Charleston, South Carolina. According to an article in the Boston *Weekly Messenger* on Nov. 14, 1833, the whip was presented to Clay by William Bates, Esq. during Clay's visit to Westfield on that day.

In addition to the article's giving attention to the gift, the fact it was printed in newspapers across the country is an early recognition of Westfield's whip industry.

1836, Daniel Webster, lawyer, U.S. Representative (N.H. & Ma.) and U.S. Senator (Ma.)

Daniel Webster's whip was manufactured by Hiram Hull's company and presented to him by the Hon. Patrick Boise during a brief visit to Westfield on Oct. 12, 1836. A Pittsfield, Ma., *Sun* newspaper article of June 13, 1833 quoted the editor of the Springfield Republican as stating, "saw the elegant whip which was made there, (with a lash nine feet long ! !) ."

1842, President John Tyler

The whip made for President John Tyler was specially designed just for him and provides an example of how special engraving not only honored the recipient, on occasion it was also a vehicle to deliver a political message. The whip was described on Sep. 29, 1842 by the *Sun* of Pittsfield, Ma. as follows:

> "One of the whip manufacturers of Westfield, a Mr. Dow, has just completed a 'Tyler Whip.' It is an invention of his own. It is a beautiful stock about 3 ½ feet long, with the name of John Tyler, Veto 1,2,3,4, inwrought in the braided cat gut in black letters. There are also four switch lashes about eighteen inches long, gracefully wrought upon the end with Silk snappers. Mr. D. intends to send it to Washington, to Mr. Tyler."

The "Veto 1, 2, 3, 4" reference was clearly an acknowledgement of Tyler's having already used his presidential veto power 4 times early in his only term as President. John Tyler would go on to use the presidential veto 10 times during his time as president. He also became the first President to have Congress override his veto of a bill on March 3, 1845.

1862, President Abraham Lincoln

Abraham Lincoln appears to be the most famous individual to have been presented with a Westfield Whip. The Springfield *Republican* on Feb. 15, 1862 reported:

> "The American whip company of Westfield have manufactured an elegant gold mounted and ivory handled whip with Union emblems and devices, which they design to present to President Lincoln. This is a hint that a little faster progress of the chariot of state would gratify the loyal people of the North."

The whip was presented to Lincoln on March 13, 1862 in a private meeting in his council chamber. Secretaries Chase and Stanton were also reported to have been in attendance. However, the presentation appears to have been brief and received less than expected attention due to the fact President Lincoln was reportedly still grieving from the recent death of his son Willie earlier in February.

1864, General Hugh Judson Kilpatrick, Civil War General

On March 25, 1864, George E. Searle was credited as being the donor of a whip described as: "An ivory handled riding whip has lately been finished by Charles Spencer of Westfield, for presentation to Gen Kilpatrick."

By any account, the presentation of a whip to Kilpatrick was an interesting choice. Hugh Judson Kilpatrick was an extremely controversial cavalry general in the Civil War and reportedly not well liked by his troops.

George E. Searle was a member of the 1st Massachusetts Cavalry and his unit may have been under the command of Kilpatrick at some point, although there is no immediate evidence to suggest that. Whatever the reason, Searle obviously must have thought highly of Kilpatrick to have a special riding whip made for him.

1869, President Ulysses S. Grant

Similar to gifts previously given to public figures, the newspapers of the day implied the gift of a pair of whips to Ulysses S. Grant would be used to curry political favors. On Thursday August 19, 1869, the Pittsfield Ma. *Sun* reported preparations for the gifting:

> "Read, Lewis & Rand of Westfield, are manufacturing at their Whip Manufactory a pair of magnificent whips intended as a present for Gen. Grant. It remains to be seen what office will be conferred upon each member of this firm!"

1892, Republican National Convention Rochester, N.Y.

A lengthy article in the New York Tribune described the Republican National Convention held on June 28, 1892, attended by about 3000 delegates. A section of the article described the whips made by American Whip.

"WHIPS FOR THE DELEGATES

> "…As each delegate entered the hall he received a small whalebone whip. To each whip were fastened a small flag and a picture of General Harrison. Alongside of the picture were the words: 'Our Candidate.' Before the convention opened the delegates amused themselves by cracking the whips at imaginary Democrats. They declared that they would carry these whips home

and whip into line enough Republicans to give Cleveland and his Free-Trade followers a good drubbing this fall. Each whip had a bright blue cracker and as the delegates sat in the hall the waving tips added greatly to the effect"……. "The whips were the gifts of American Whip Company of Westfield, Mass. They are of American made and many Republican farmers will urge their horses toward the ballot box on election day with these republican whips….."

Labor

One question often asked is - Where did the labor pool come from to satisfy the needs of the growing industry? The early 1800's was well before the waves of immigrants who would arrive later in the century. Also, while Westfield was growing, it was not increasing in size on a par with some of the larger cities in the region such as Springfield, Worcester and Hartford, Connecticut.

However, the lack of competing industries provided Westfield with a previously untapped pool of resources, namely women. The whip industry afforded employment to women and as statistics will prove later, many of the larger firms had more female employees than men.

The braiding of lashes and snaps was commonly done by many women in their homes as a cottage industry allowing for their part time employment without needing to sacrifice their roles at home. There are many accounts in personal diaries of women making a few dozen or more lashes at a time, which would be delivered to one of the whip makers,

In *Westfield Massachusetts, 1669-1969,* the chapter 'Old Industry' by Patrick Flahive, describes entries from the diary of Aurelia Taylor where she referred to making lashes on almost a daily basis. The entries from early December of 1832, described her as typically braiding 2-3 dozen lashes daily for Hiram Hull. Her entries described returning lashes and receiving a similar amount or more.

The wording of "returning lashes and receiving a similar amount or more" was possibly meant to convey she was actually braiding snaps to attach to the ends of lashes already braided in the shop.

Given that Hull's shop required many more than the 2-3 dozen whips per day accounted for by Aurelia Taylor, he would have engaged many women to perform this role. As the whip shops grew in size and whip production increased, women continued to braid lashes and snaps throughout the remainder of the century.

The fact that braiding lashes and snaps could be done from home also allowed women in surrounding communities to work for the local Westfield shops expanding the available pool of resources even more. One example being Cynthia Loomis Dayton of Blandford. The personal diaries of her husband Giles Dayton in the 1870's have several entries where he delivered lashes to Westfield for work his wife Cynthia had completed.

While there are many known examples of women performing these tasks, it will never truly be known how many women were involved. However, it is clear there were hundreds of women braiding lashes and snaps at home over several decades through much of the middle to late 1800's.

With the women working at home, often on part time basis, they were prone to being overlooked when accounting for the number of people employed in the whip industry. This is one possible explanation for the wide variance in statistics regarding the number of people employed as working on whips. Surveys typically accounted only for those people working within the shops and factories versus outside the shops, potentially overlooking this vital statistic.

While many women worked from home, a substantial number also worked inside the whip factories. One of the earliest documented whip related labor issues in Westfield's whip industry involved the women employees of the J.R. Rand Whip Co. On April 20, 1861 a Springfield *Republican* newspaper article reported:

> "Twenty girls employed in J.R. Rand's whip factory, at Westfield, struck and marched the streets in procession, It has been due them for a long time."

Another newspaper report of Sept. 7, 1865,

> "The girls employed in the whip and cigar shops at Westfield struck for higher wages successfully last week. The cigar girls had their pay raised $1 per week, and the whip makers met in convention and adopted a uniform scale of prices which will no doubt prove satisfactory all around."

One of the reasons for the labor unrest with the female employees was undoubtedly the discrepancies in compensation compared to their male peers. The *1865 State of Massachusetts Report on Industry* clearly shows the whip companies were paying their female employees on average about one third of amount earned by the male workers. While a portion of this gap may have been because of the type jobs each performed, it illustrates how female workers were certainly compensated at a much lower rate than their male counterparts.

The 'Schedules of Manufactures' (1850) and 'Products of Industry Schedules' (1860) of the U.S. Federal Censuses reported wage statistics having similar pay discrepancies between males and female employees. The 1880 Federal Census records recorded statistics differentiating between skilled mechanics and ordinary workers. While not gender specific, it is very unlikely many (if any) women were included in the skilled mechanic category. The ordinary workers were typically paid 50-60% less than a skilled mechanic.

One of the more creative attempts to overcome this discrepancy was documented in a newspaper article of 1856 in the Springfield *Republican* which was carried in many of the major newspapers across the country. The article read:

> " PANTALOONS vs. PETTICOATS – a young woman has been working in the factory of the American Whip Company, at Westfield, during the last six months attired in male clothes. She pretended to be a nice young man of 17, smoked large Havanas made at Feeding Hills, and acted her part as a modern gentleman very well to all outside appearances."

The article was later expanded upon to include a report that the same female had also disguised herself in the same manner previously in New York.

As with other industries, labor issues would continue to exist well into the 1900's prior to the establishment of unions. However, even as other industries were successfully establishing unions, the whip employees were never able to successfully unionize for any extended period in the 1800's.

Creation of a union structure was hampered by a couple basic reasons. First, there were only a couple firms with a large enough employee base to establish an organized body of workers. Additionally, with the whip industry being over 50% of the organized industry in Westfield, the opportunities for seeking employment in other industries were limited. Another contributing factor was, that in addition to owning the whip companies, several of the same individuals also ran the Cigar factories, Westfield's other major industry having similar pay structures. Thus, as long as the whip shops cooperated with each other, they could successfully mandate the wages and control the bulk of the workers.

Despite several attempts, a sustained labor union does not appear to have been achievable. The *1895 Massachusetts Annual Reports on Public Officers and Institutions* made note of the Whip Makers Union having been disbanded due to its having been ineffective. According to newspaper articles the union had only been in existence for slightly over 2 years before being disbanded.

In another attempt, the Whip Makers Protective Union No. 9434 was established prior to 1901 when it was listed in the *Massachusetts Labor Bulletin of 1901*. Wm. M. Cowles of 8 Madison St was listed as the head of the organization. How long that union existed is unclear but it appears to have been abandoned after a few years. In 1916 newspaper articles were again reporting attempts to organize the whip-makers but those attempts also do not appear to have been successful.

Commemorative ribbon from the Whip Makers Protective Union

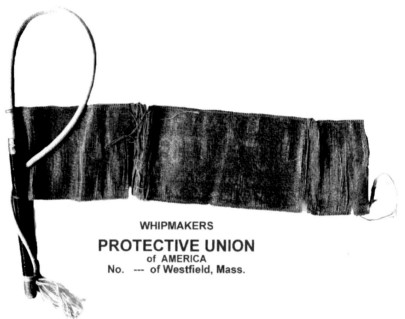

Courtesy Westfield Athenaeum, Westfield, Ma.

Convict Labor

One of the more interesting and controversial practices regarding labor was the use of convict labor by some whip companies.

Beginning in June of 1853, Hiram Hull & Co. contracted with the Massachusetts state prison in Charlestown to have 67 convicts manufacture whips for his company. According to an 1854 report, Hiram Hull & Co. was one of seven companies employing a total of 350 convicts in a variety of industries having contracts of 5 years, with beginning dates ranging from 1850-1854. The largest company employing convict labor in Charlestown was the company of Forester, Lawrence & Co. having four contracts with a total of 161 men engaged in: Upholstery (56), Cabinet Making (52), Varnishing (22) and Carving (31).

Hiram Hull's oldest son, Liverus, relocated to Charleston to oversee the whip operations. Liverus' younger brother David subsequently joined him with running the whip shop. When Hiram Hull, Hiram Harrison and Samuel Dow merged their firms establishing American Whip, the Hull brothers continued in their roles under the new company.

The use of convict labor caused much concern with the whip manufacturers locally. Newspaper articles were blaming American Whip's use of the convict labor with causing severe damage to the local whip industry and Westfield's overall economy. The local whip makers claimed the cheap labor used by American Whip was prohibiting them from competing, resulting in cutting back production and necessitating a reduction in the number of hands employed. This in turn was having negative effects on other businesses due to the corresponding drop in business activity.

The controversy over the inequity of wages paid to convicts, pressure from the other local whip companies and a changing political climate ultimately led to the contract not being renewed in 1868. After three successive, five-year contracts, the relationship was terminated with American Whip returning all whip manufacturing and associated labor to Westfield.

One impact of American Whip having terminated their Charleston prison operations was highlighted by a Springfield *Republican* newspaper article on Oct. 26, 1868 reporting a shortage of housing as follows:

> "There is great demand for tenements at Westfield, owing to the American Whip Co. transferring their manufacturing from the Charleston prison to that town and employing civilian mechanics. One man who advertised a home to rent received 20 applications the first day."

In spite of holding many patents for whip machines and manufacturing, Liverus Hull did not return to Westfield to rejoin American Whip. By 1868, he had already served one term as the mayor of Charleston. Shortly after the convict labor was terminated, Liverus transferred ownership of his patents to American Whip having decided to remain in Charlestown. Liverus went on establish a company making metal bedsprings. He later relocated to Chicago for the remainder of his professional career. While he retained a significant financial investment in American Whip, he did not return to live in Westfield until much later in life, when he lived out his last two years, passing away there on May 2, 1894.

David C. Hull did return to Westfield and remained integrally involved with American Whip and United States Whip Co. for the rest of his life.

American Whip wasn't the only whip company to engage in the use of convict labor. Wells Whip Co. of Wellsville, Pennsylvania is another example of a whip shop engaging with a prison for convict labor. George Powell's *1907*

History of York County, Pa. includes an accounting of the firm using convict labor in the Trenton New Jersey State prison under a contract for several years. Wells Whip also had a branch factory in Pittsburg during the Civil War. In addition to the prison labor, Wells Whip appears to have used boys from a reform school during the civil war. According to the Powell account, Wells Whip lost about 60 men due to enlistments during the war and "were compelled to employ boys from the Pennsylvania House of Refuge." Wells Whip's factory at Pittsburgh was discontinued in 1865 and no further mention of using prison or reform school labor was noted.

In 1877, Weaver and Bardall Co. of Pittsburgh entered a contract with the Moundsville, West Virginia Penitentiary for 60 hands at 25 cents per day. Of significant note is that even though it is 10 years after American's contract expired Weaver and Bardwell was paying even lower wages than American was reported as paying earlier.

By 1879 Weaver and Bardall Co. had become Weaver and Bardwell & Co. On Feb 1, 1879, the *National Labor Tribune* of Pittsburgh reported that the Moundsville West Virginia Penitentiary had issued a contract,

> "To Weaver & Bardwell, whip manufacturers formerly of Pittsburgh, Pa., about sixty hands at 25 cents per day; contract expires Aug 13, 1881…."

The contract amount appears have been renegotiated to 40 cents per day, still less than the American Whip contract of 1863. Weaver and Bardwell would continue its use of convict labor through at least 1888. Ultimately, Weaver and Bardwell would encounter similar accusations as those levelled against American Whip for using unfair cheap labor, resulting in a similar controversy arising from those contracts. By 1890 Weaver and Bardwell had ceased using convict labor for the manufacture of whips.

Fires & Floods

Fires

Fires were a constant source of concern throughout the 1800's. Towards the end of the century, as firefighting equipment improved, fires became less of an issue. It was also towards the end of the century that buildings began being outfitted with sprinkler systems, significantly reducing the damage should a fire ignite.

While fire caused significant damage in many cases, their reports are often beneficial to historians due to the additional information provided beyond simply the damage and financial loss incurred. The newspaper accounts often provided information such as the precise location of the factory, the type of manufacturing they were engaged with, partners & companies they were supplying goods to and other important demographic data not reported in other sources.

When considering the financial impact from a fire, it is important to understand how that related to the values of that time. As an example, $5,000 in 1850 would equate to almost $150,000 in 2018 dollars. As can be seen, insurance often failed to adequately cover the financial loss and sometimes not at all.

A few articles on some of the more significant fires to the Westfield whip shops follow. Except where otherwise noted the information was extracted from the *Springfield Republic* of Springfield, Massachusetts.

Hiram Hull, Aug 13, 1835

The *Hampshire Gazette*, Northampton, Ma reported that a two story building owned and occupied by Hiram Hull and David Johnson was destroyed by fire. The building was described as containing: "a turning shop, carding machine, fulling mill, machine shop and c." The fire was reported to have been caused by friction from a grunion with the lost estimated as being between $3,000 and $4,000.

Hial Holcomb, Jan 20, 1852

"whip factory at West Parish, large quantity of whips value $800-900, insured for $450."

West Parish being the section of Westfield currently known as Mundale.

Richard Furrows, Mar 4, 1852

"Richard Furrows whip factory in Westfield was consumed by fire last week.... The entire loss is upwards of $2,000. The following persons are the sufferers from this fire: Richard Furrow, building and tools $700; Dow & Co., $600; E. Sizer, $300; C. Mallory, $100; H. Harrison & Co., $50; S. Pulsifer, $150; Morand & Co. $60; Lamberton & Swan, $20; J. & R. Noble, $50"

This account provides an early glimpse into how some whip related companies became more specialized as 'jobbers' to other concerns. Richard Furrow primarily manufactured whip stocks for the larger concerns. Furrow is also an example of how individuals would often only operate in the industry for short periods. In the 1855 Massachusetts state census his occupation was still listed as a whip maker. However, by 1860, the US Federal Census listed his occupation as a farmer. Subsequent state and federal census' would continue to report the same. His death record in 1877 also reported his occupation as a farmer.

Rand & Co., July 12, 1853

In a widely reported accounting, the Jasper R. Rand whip factory burned on July 12, 1853. In part the newspaper accounts described the fire as follows:

"The large wood building known as 'Rand's Whip factory' in Westfield was discovered to be on fire at 7 o'clock Monday evening"....... "Loss was about $5000 with building insured for $800 and stock for $2,500"...... "The fire was discovered when all hands were absent from the building for supper and probably originated in the chimney".

A theme often observed in these accounts was the fact a large percentage of the fires occurred 'off hours' for a variety of reasons. Regardless of the initial cause, the lack of fire alarms or sprinkler systems allowed even small fires to build beyond what might have been to a minor issue during the day when people were still in the building.

Franklin Arthur, Mar 7, 1855

The following article from the *Springfield Republican* described a fire which destroyed several buildings including a whip shop and the fact it was a total financial loss due to a defunct insurance policy.

> "Fire in Westfield – On Wednesday afternoon, the buildings of Franklin Arthur in Little River, about 3 miles from the center of Westfield, were discovered to be on fire, and before the engines could arrive, the house, whip shops, barn and sheds were nearly if not entirely destroyed, at a heavy loss, including $1200 worth of whips. His Insurance amounts to $1000, unfortunately in a defunct Western Office."

Discovery of this article led to deeper research into the fact Franklin Arthur was one of the earlier whip makers in Westfield. However, Franklin Arthur, like some other early whip makers, is not mentioned in any of the historical summaries on Westfield's whip industry which have been published by multiple historians.

Interestingly, research on Arthur Franklin led to uncovering information on the exact location of his house and the fact it is currently owned by Dennis Picard a well-known local historian. For more details see Arthur Franklin in the chapter on Early Whip Makers.

Lester Holcomb & Co., destroyed May 14, 1861

Incendiary fires from vandals, disgruntled ex-employees or other suspicious reasons were not uncommon. Once again, with the lack of fire alarms or sprinklers, a vandal could start a small fire and escape well before anybody would observe the growing fire being heavily engaged. One example being the fire of Lester Holcomb & Co.

> "The whip manufactory in Westfield near the Great River mills of Ira Yeamans, Jr was destroyed by an incendiary fire early Tuesday, together with all the machinery and a large number of whips ready for market…..loss is about $10,000, on which there is insurance of $3500. …establishment to be rebuilt immediately."

Van Deusen Bros, Oct. 8, 1866

Another example of an after-hours fire was that of the Van Deusen Bros. factory which was located near the intersection of Bartlett and Mechanic Streets adjacent to what is now an underground stream crossing Mechanic Street just south of that intersection.

> "The whip manufactory of Van Deusen brothers on Mechanic Street at Westfield was burned on Monday evening. Much of the stock was saved but the machinery and a large amount of whalebone was destroyed......"

A subsequent article stated final loss at $29,500 which was fully insured.

American Whip, total loss May 7, 1869

In multiple articles across the country it was reported that the entire Main Street block of the American Whip building was destroyed by fire. Different estimates put the loss at $75,000-80,000 with approximately one half of that being insured. The article also noted 125 hands were put out of work.

One of the more interesting notes regarding the fire was a subsequent article reporting the cause of the fire as being caused by rats gnawing on matches which they had brought back to their nest. The nest containing debris and oily rags supplied the fuel for the fire to grow.

American Whip used manufacturing space rented from the A. & D. Avery Co. to run nights until their factory was completely rebuilt at the same location several months later in September of the same year.

E.B. Light Whip Company & Avery Whip Co., Nov. 23, 1870

The former Hampden Cigar building experienced a major fire of suspicious origin which affected many whip companies. The building owned by Albert T. Rand of New York and located on the east side of Elm Street was totally destroyed by the fire.

The E.B. Light Co. located on the first floor was able to successfully remove much of their goods and the remainder was covered by insurance. However, the A. & D. Avery Co. located on the upper floors suffered major losses. The Avery's were machinists and general jobbers, plaiting whips for various whip companies in town and suffered significant losses estimated at $16,000, including 42 plaiting machines; insured for $10,000. The newspaper article continued on to state that Westfield Whip lost $1000 in goods and Smith and

Darling, $2000. The news articles noted that almost every whip manufacturer in town had whips there, ranging in value from $100 to $800, with none of the goods being insured.

An interesting side note of suspicious nature is that the newspaper article gave an accounting that the Avery's were in the process of purchasing the building from the Rand family. Reportedly, the day before the fire they had forwarded a copy of the property to A. D. Rand in New York for his signature to transfer ownership to the Avery's. As a result of the fire, the agreement was never consummated.

Ironically, the Avery factory was the one rented by American Whip the previous year while their own factory was being rebuilt, after the fire of May 7, 1869.

W.W. Richardson explosion, fire & fatality, Jul. 13, 1873

As noted before, many whip company fires were after hours when the employees had already left for the day. As a result, injuries were not frequently encountered or reported. The Richardson fire of 1873 is a notable exception. W.W. Richardson had leased a section of one of H.B. Smith's buildings on Main St. to manufacture whip buttons.

On the evening of June 13th, there was an explosion in an oven. In addition to putting half the building in ruins, his son, William A. Richardson, age 21, was killed. Also injured in the fire was Albert Longley who tripped over a hose and broke his leg.

The loss to Richardson amounted to $3,000 while E.S. Miller's lash manufactory and two other unrelated businesses were a total loss. Total loss for the fire was $10,000 which was partially insured.

Westfield Power Co. Bldg. / Peck & Whipple, Nov 7, 1884

The fire in the stock room of the Peck & Whipple Whip Co. caused an estimated total of $18,000 damage of which $15,000 was suffered by Peck & Whipple. There was $2,000 worth of damage to the building and a minor damage to some other occupants amounting to less than $1,000.

Osden Whip factory burns, Feb. 5, 1891,

The Osden Whip factory located on Little River off Granville Road in Mundale burned on February 5, 1891. The mill known as the "Ruinsville Mill" was the last significant whip factory outside of the central whip district in

Westfield. Aside from a few small shops, all whip manufacturing in Westfield had by this time become centralized in the downtown district.

San Francisco Earthquake/Fire Disaster 1906

While not a Westfield Event, the 1906 San Francisco disaster affected the well-known Atwater family of Westfield.

David Atwater had relocated to San Francisco in 1881. After building a successful whip business there, lost both his home and business in which he had everything invested to the earthquake/fire.

Ensign Box / A.J. Cook Whip Company, 2 Fires 1907

The Ensign Box factory on Cherry Street. in which the A.J. Cook Whip company was also located, suffered two fires in the spring/summer of 1907.

The first fire was on Mar. 9, 1907 at about 6:00 P.M. While the fire was contained quickly with 5 streams of water, the newspapers reported the loss caused by water damage was greater than the fire itself. After the fire was thought to have been extinguished, a watchman sent in a second alarm at about 1:00 A.M. for a small fire near the filling room. The building itself was not heavily damaged with the greatest amount of loss due to the stock and other contents. Loss due to the fire/water was estimated at approximately $30,000-$40,000.

The second fire on July 26, 1907 was only slightly less in terms of losses than the March fire. Initially estimated at $20,000 the amount of damage was later given as close to $30,000.

Floods

While not as prevalent as fires, flooding was also a concern for many whip shops. With many early shops located near streams and rivers for power, occasional flooding was a concern as it was for Grist Mills, Saw Mills and other shops.

Additionally, the Elm Street area between Franklin Street and the Great River Bridge (a.k.a. Green Bridge) had a large number of whip shops and was prone to significant flooding on several occasions in the 1800's and early 1900's. It wasn't until an adequate dyke system was developed to alleviate the problem with the banks of the Westfield River overflowing, that the ongoing flooding became less of a concern.

The most significant flood affecting multiple whip shops was the flood of Dec. 10, 1878, which caused massive damage to Westfield in general and the downtown area of Elm, Franklin and Mechanic Streets in particular. The damage to the whip district was due to the banks of the river upstream from the Great River bridge overflowing into the downtown area. Initially the damage to the town was estimated at $200,000-$300,00 but was later adjusted to be closer to $500,000.

The flood damage was of such significance that reports of it were published in many of the newspapers across the country. The Boston *Daily Advertiser* was one of the major newspapers which reported the flood damage in detail. on December 12, 1878

Excerpts from its' Dec 10th article specifically relating to the whip shops include:

> "the buildings destroyed were mostly in the vicinity of downstream, in the direct path of the flood".… "Peck, Osden & Co.'s factory is also gone, including the brick storeroom. The damage to the stock alone is $5,000. Leonard Atwater's unoccupied whip factory, Provin's four-story brick block and E. Avery's whip factory are all smashed to pieces"… "Provin's block was worth $10,000. Two wooden whip factories, occupied by Holcomb & Cook and Edmund Cooper were swept away with all their contents" … "A. C. Barnes, living at Shepherd Street had his house split in two and his whip shop carried away into another man's yard, his loss $1500."

The S. A. Allen Power Building was located at the Great River Bridge perched on the bank of the Westfield River where it could be utilized to generate power. A such, it was particularly susceptible to flooding caused by ice jams and high water from the Westfield River.

On Mar. 1, 1896, a sudden flood caused by an ice jam, caused significant damage to that building and was described in the Springfield *Republican* on May 3, 1869 as:

> "The damage caused by the flooding of Pomeroy & Van Deusen's stock room at their whip factory is heavy, and Mr. Van Deusen said the concerns loss would probably not be under $3,000."

The Van Deusen Whip building, as the S.A. Allen Building came to be known. suffered similar damage on Apr 21, 1901 when the Westfield River once again flooded the basement storage area of the Van Deusen Whip factory.

Similar to what had occurred in 1896, the flooding caused a substantial amount of damage to their stock. When Van Deusen Whip relocated to Arnold Street in 1917, while not explicitly stated, the ongoing issues with water flooding the building was likely one of the factors prompting the move.

The building continued to encounter damage from floods including 1927, 1936 and finally 1938 which dealt the final blow, severely damaging the building beyond repair causing it to be condemned and the remains demolished.

Patents

Another often asked question is - 'How did Westfield maintain so much control over the whip industry?' The manufacturing base, available financial resources and available labor pool were certainly significant factors.

Unquestionably, Westfield's control of significant portions of the patents for whip related inventions was also a key contributor to Westfield's dominance and control.

Research for this book uncovered 349 patents identified as being whip related from 1808 to 1920. 156 of these (or approximately 44%) are assigned to Westfield.

Several factors indicate there are likely additional patents which to date have not been identified. The first issue was a major fire on Dec. 15,1836 at the Washington, D.C. patent office when approximately 10,000 patents records and models were lost. Of this, almost 3000 were able to be restored. The patents for the remaining 7000 were cancelled.

In 1847, the Patent Office published *A list of Patents for Invention and Designs issued by the United States for the years 1790 to 1847.* documenting the earliest patents. While a significant number of the patent submission letters and models were lost and detailed information is not available, this document provides a reference to many of the earliest patents whose detailed records were destroyed in the 1836 fire.

Research uncovered 5 whip patents from 1836 and previous years, related to whips but it is possible a few more exist which were not recovered and were cancelled.

Also, during the early years of the industry, the patent office hadn't established whip categories. The earliest patent discovered under a whip specific category was in 1842.

Another challenge to identifying whip patents is that even after the whip categories were established, many patents, particularly those for machines, were filed in categories not normally associated with whip making. Since the uses for some machines spanned several industries, it was not in the best interest of an inventor to limit his description to being solely a 'whip invention'. In many cases, the title's description and detailed specifications identified them as being whip related in addition to other uses. Filing it in a broader category such as textile braiders, cutting machines, lathes, etc. offered them more protection than a narrower classification would have. One example of this would have been a device used for turning whip stocks. Rather than defining it as a whip machine, it would have been filed as a lathe to cover its possible use in woodworking or metal works. While the logic for doing this is understandable, it creates a challenge to someone doing research of this nature.

The texts of patent descriptions and diagrams vary widely with each submission. Some are very brief with simple diagrams while others are very detailed with complex diagrams. In addition to the patent description being beneficial to understanding the new invention or improvement, it also provides other details to assist with uncovering related patents. The text often identifies previous patents being improved upon, dates, people's names and their locations. These additional details assisted with expanding not only the list of known patents but also with developing a better understanding of the evolution of the industry.

To better understand Westfield's control of patents during the growth years of the industry, patents prior to 1900 were reviewed in greater detail. That refined focus revealed 285 patents applying to the whip industry. Of these items, 141 were directly accredited to Westfield area residents with another 14 credited to Hiram Hull in Charlestown, Ma. As noted previously, Liverus Hull, a Westfield native and son of Hiram Hull, was running the convict whip shop at the state prison for the Hiram Hull Whip Company of Westfield and later American Whip. As such, Hull's patents are actually Westfield controlled patents. When combined with the previously identified Westfield patents, the total for Westfield patents becomes 155. The combined total for Westfield places it as being over 54% of the overall whip patents.

However, a closer examination of the whip patent classifications provides a better perspective on the more critical patents important to Westfield's control of the industry.

Whip Patent classification structure

Within the US patent classifications, whips are assigned a classification code of '231'. Under that code there are multiple sub-categories for various aspects of whip making as shown below.

US Patent Office Classification Code 231 and sub-classes
Sub Class:
- 1   Whip Machines
- 2.1 Whip
- 3   Convertible whips and canes
- 4   Lashes
- 5   Lash and snap fastenings
- 6   Caps, Buttons and Joints
- 7   Electric Prod

The sub-categories most important for the core manufacturing processes of whip making are machines and those for the core whips.

The sub-categories for Lashes, Sockets/Holders, Whip racks and other accessories were less important to the core processes of the industry.

With this in mind, the sub-categories of machines (1), and whip (2.1) combined with patents for whip-related machines filed under 'non-whip' categories are the patents most important to controlling the overall industry.

When theses parameters are considered there are 203 patents issued prior to 1900 which are applicable to the core manufacturing processes. Of these 203 patents, 121 were controlled by Westfield whip firms.

As such, almost 60% of the most important patents fell under the control of Westfield.

Earliest Whip Patent

While Westfield became the hub for the whip industry in the United States, the first patent found for a whalebone whip wasn't from Westfield. In addition to its being a whalebone whip, it was the earliest whip related patent of any type found during this research.

The aforementioned patent office report covering 1790 to 1847, lists a patent on Nov 25, 1808 assigned to Joseph Reeve of Newburg, New York. The patent for making whips was simply titled: "Whip, twisted, whalebone".

An advertisement in the *Rights of Man* newspaper of Newburgh, New York dated Sept 3, 1804 describes Joseph Reeves, Gold & Silversmith, Whip and Watch Maker. Amongst his articles for sale are 'Loaded Whalebone Whips of the best Quality' and 'Raw Hide Whips.'

A subsequent advertisement regarding Joseph Reeves in the *Bee* of Hudson, N.Y on December 6, 1808. includes the text:

> "The Subscriber informs the public that he has procured a patent from the President of the United States, dated the 25th of April 1808 for making twisted Whale-Bone, Horse, Chair, and Carriage Whips."

Communication with the U.S. Patent Office confirmed their records have Joseph Reeves as the owner and document the patent date as Nov. 25th in agreement with the published report of 1847. While, this conflicts with the Apr. 25th date in the newspaper article, the official patent office documents support

Joseph Reeve's having the first whip whalebone patent. Further research didn't uncover Newburg(h), New York having any whip factories or significant involvement in the whip industry. Other than the patent office list and the newspaper advertisements, no reference to Joseph Reeves or any connection to known whip factories has been found.

The historical significance of this patent is that it not only pre-dates any documented whip patents for Westfield, it also pre-dates Westfield's use of whalebone in whip making by approximately fourteen years. As patents of this era had a term of fourteen years, the gap is important because the patent would have expired in 1822, very close to when Hiram Hull acquired the whip machine patent rights from Thorpe.

The combination of Reeve's patent expiring, enabling others to use whalebone in whips, combined with Hulls acquiring the patent rights to Thorpe's machine at around the same time, set the stage for Westfield being able to leverage both events in growing its fledgling industry.

Westfield's Earliest Patents

The first two patents uncovered as being attributable to the Westfield whip industry were both issued on Apr. 27, 1932.

The first patent, numbered x7.107, assigned as being from Westfield was granted to Giles Dayton of Blandford and Andrew Mallory of Russell, titled 'Whip Engine for turning Whip Stocks.' The 'Whip Engine' was basically a specially designed lathe for turning whip stocks (stocks being another name for handles.)

On the same date as the Dayton/Mallory patent, Fred Morgan of Westfield received one for "Applying Varnish to Whips". The patent is listed in the patent office report listing patents issued from 1790 to 1847. Unfortunately, while the 1790-1847 Patent Office document lists Morgan's name, the title description and issue date, it doesn't include additional information such as its assignment number. This patent is one of the documents lost in the US Patent Office fire and no further details exist.

On a personal note, Giles Dayton was the 4th great grandfather of the author of this work. While our family was aware of his being a 'mechanic' working on machinery related to grist mills, saw mills and related equipment, the discovery of his owning this early patent was a revelation to the family.

The text of the patent submission letter consists of two pages of detailed information describing how to position the stock during the turning process. The lathe is shown in the following diagram submitted with the patent application. The category for this patent was simply a 'lathe' as it predates any whip specific categories having been established.

The following diagram is part of the submission letter sent to the US Patent office for the Dayton/Mallory Whip Engine.

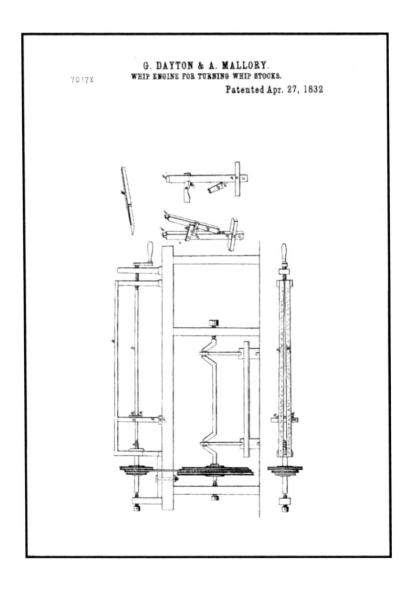

The next Westfield whip related patent was for Enos and Nelson Alvord on Oct. 11, 1836. Labelled a 'Lathe for Turning & C.', the description is another example of how many machines were broadly described beyond just their uses for whip making. As stated previously, this gave broader protection to the patent holder for a variety of industries. The description in part stated:

> " a new and improved machine or lathe adapted to the turning of a great variety of articles, both large and small, whether they are required to be cylindrical or regularly tapered or to be bulged or swelled in one or more parts -such for example as gaffs for the sails of vessels, whip-stocks, ramrods, etc......."

While, it isn't explicitly stated, this patent was likely possibly filed at this time to establish the rights to their improved lathe since the patent of 14 years for the Dayton/Mallory device had just expired.

First Westfield Patent for a Whip Braiding machine

The first Westfield patent for an improvement to a braiding machine was Seymour Halliday's patent of Apr 4, 1838.

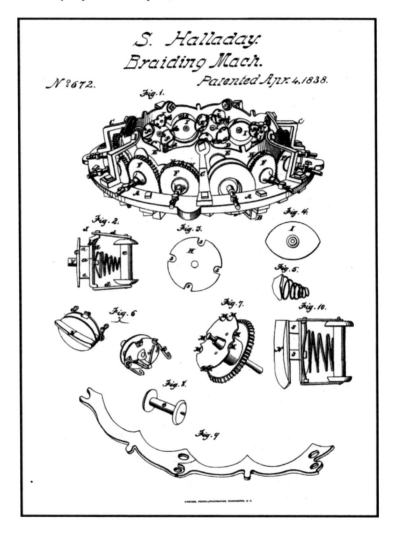

Halladay's patent was described as an improvement to Thorp's machine. The patent diagram shows the detail of the plaiting machine which has a circular rotating mechanism for weaving the braiding material. The general concept of this type of mechanism is the basis for the machines to follow for much of the 1800's.

While the Halladay machine greatly improved the plaiting process, whip making was still manually intensive and this device only improved one of the numerous steps.

The Dayton/Mallory, Morgan, Alvord and Halladay patents are just four in a long list of Westfield based patents which would dominate the industry for the rest of the nineteenth century.

Westfield Men with the most patents

Of the patents which have been uncovered, the Westfield men who either owned or co-owned the most patents are as follows:

Liverus Hull *	14
David C. Hull	12
Henry Mullen	11
James Noble, Jr.	8
Addison C. Rand	8
Charles C. Pratt	7
Henry J Bush	6
John J. Bohler	6
Gamaliel King	5
Henry M. Van Deusen	5
Dexter Avery	5
Frederick Couse	4
Charles G. Becker	4
Elkinah Ring	4
John C. Schmidt	4

* While running the whip operations for American Whip in the Charlestown state prison.

It's important to note that in addition to introducing the first true braiding machines, the Hull family extended its influence over the industry by virtue of owning an additional 26 whip patents extending from 1855 to 1911.

Interestingly, Hiram Hull, regarded by many as the father of Westfield's whip industry did not hold any patents himself. The Hull family patents were all held by his son's Liverus and David. Additionally, none of the Hull patents were co-owned by the brothers. It is likely that they worked on the early inventions together while running the whip shop in the Charlestown prison, with the early patents all filed under Liverus' name. This is possibly an acknowledgement of his position in the company and seniority over his younger brother David. Liverus' patents were also all filed prior to 1870. David C. Hull's patents began in 1872 after Liverus had left the business and David had returned to Westfield.

James Noble Jr. received credit for on a total of 12 patents, 8 as co-owner and 4 by virtue of being the assignor. However, he was not the sole owner of a single patent. Seven of the patents were co-owned with Henry Mullen and one with George E. Whipple. He was named as an assignor on an additional three by Elkinah Ring and one more by William Morse. On that patent, Morse designated Henry Mullen and James Noble Jr. two-thirds owners. It is probable James Noble Jr was only a co-owner of these patents as a representative of Westfield Whip and later American Whip, companies for which he was an officer. Henry Mullen had another 4 patents in his own name.

Addison C. Rand had a total of 8 patents attributable to him. While fourth highest amongst the Westfield men, all 8 were registered in the two year period of May 5, 1868 to May 10, 1870. With the Rand family exiting the whip business by 1871, it appears Addison had been planning for the end of the company's business for some time. With patents having a term of 14 years, at the time of Addison Rand leaving Westfield in 1871, he still retained the rights for all of his patents for another 11-13 years.

The patent descriptions are also important in assisting with the identification of which men concentrated on the whip materials, methods of construction, machines, lashes or other specialized functions.

It is also important to note that while the Westfield men who held the patents can be identified, they were often the owners of the shops or representatives of the firms. In many cases, especially for the larger firms, the men who actually made the improvements or at the very least made a considerable contribution to the invention were not documented and have unfortunately been lost to history.

A full listing of Westfield area residents holding patents with patent numbers, dates and title/brief description is included in the Appendices.

Early Era (1810-1855)

Westfield's whip industry had its birth shortly after 1800. Some early accounts credit Titus Pease and Thomas Rose having begun making whips in 1801. Many other accounts assign credit for the earliest making of whips to a 'Joseph Jokes' in 1808.

Joseph Jokes

Research of census records, old land deeds and other resources failed to uncover any reference to a Joseph Jokes or anyone of a similar name as being connected to Westfield. It is possible Jokes was only in Westfield a short period thus avoiding any census records or other reasons for having his activities documented. However, the same sources who attribute Jokes as the founder of the whip industry, also describe him as owning a plot of choice hickory. It was also stated he made whips for his neighbors after having made whips for himself. These statements would imply he would have resided in Westfield for a longer period. However, again, a search of census records, tax records, vital statistics & property deeds have failed to uncovered any firm documentation regarding his existence.

Given the fact Joseph Jokes has thus far been unable to be verified as a real person and acknowledging Westfield's desire to establish itself as the hub of the development of the whip industry, the possibility arises that Joseph Jokes making whips in the 1808 timeframe may very possibly have been a fabrication or a composite created to represent the earliest whip makers. Whether Joseph Jokes was an actual person or is simply representative of one or more people who made whips for themselves or others around this time will likely never be proven or disproven.

The difficulty confirming the existence of Joseph Jokes is typical of tracing other early whip makers of Westfield. Confirmation of individuals as having been whip makers is complicated by the fact that making whips was often a supplemental activity to their primary occupation of farming.

There are numerous references to men whose obituaries or newspaper accounts described them as being early whip makers although census records, marriage records and death notices typically described them as farmers.

Titus Pease

At stated previously, some early accounts credit Titus Pease and Thomas Rose with having started making whips around 1801. While both are known to have been Westfield residents, aside from stories handed down for several generations and published in historical accounts written many years later, little is known about Thomas Rose having made whips, while there is more information available about Titus Pease.

Titus Pease has been described as having lived in the Little River section of town and early deeds appear to confirm that fact. The Pease family occupied several parcels on Little River Road, including at least one parcel later owned by Franklin Arthur, although the exact location of Titus' house hasn't been fully confirmed.

One confirmation regarding Titus Pease as a whip maker comes from the genealogical history titled, *The Dows or Dowse Family in America*. In that work, the marriage of Hannah Morse (nee) of Waltham, Ma. and Titus Pease of Westfield is documented. Furthermore, it's the second marriage of each. Hannah's first marriage to Lyman Ryan stated he was a whip-maker in Waltham and 'prob.' born in Westfield. Her second marriage to Titus Pease states he was also a whip-maker. The Waltham, Ma. Vital Records confirm the marriage of Mrs. Hannah Ryan to Titus Pease of Westfield in 1831. No confirmation that Lyman Ryan was actually born in Westfield has been found.

Another reference to a 'Mr. Pease of Little River' was included within a biographical sketch of Hiram Harrison Lee in the *Encyclopedia of Massachusetts, Genealogical – Biographical Review*, published in 1916. The sketch also included several paragraphs about his father-in-law Charles W. Spencer. Charles W. Spencer who was born in 1813, is noted as having served a two year apprenticeship to Pease beginning at the age of 18, placing both him and Pease at Little River in 1831. C. W. Spencer would go on to a long whip making career of over 5 decades before retiring from the business in 1889.

Titus Pease died in Westfield on Apr. 22, 1844. Similar to many of the early whip makers, Massachusetts vital records for his death reported his occupation as being a farmer.

Samuel Lindsey

A *Westfield Times Newsletter* article of Aug. 21, 1851 gives credit to Samuel Lindsay (Lindsey) for commencing the whip business in a small whip shop on the corner of Broad and Silver Streets some forty years previous (c. 1811), with Joel Farnum following soon afterward on Elm Street where the Lewis block stood. The article describes the whips of Lindsay and Farnum as being "a very cheap article, being twisted wooden stalks covered with leather."

What differentiated Lindsey and Farnum from other early whip makers is that they appear to have been the first to establish shops for making whips located 'in town' versus the outlying farms where whips were initially made.

The premise that Samuel Lindsey operated an early whip shop on the corner of Broad and Silver Streets is supported by several documents. In 1809, a deed has him purchasing the tract of land on the corner of Broad and West Silver Streets. In a subsequent deed of 1826, when Joel took a mortgage on that same parcel from Abner Post, he is described as being a whip maker. The federal census records of 1840 listed him as a farmer. However, the 1855 Massachusetts State Census and Westfield Vital records for 1858 when he died both list his occupation as whip maker.

Joel Farnum

Joel Farnham was a partner of Benjamin Hastings in trade as retailers and partners in multiple land transactions. The two of them are named together in over 50 deeds for parcels of land, mills, and farms between 1800 and 1818 spread across several areas of Westfield.

It appears that Farnham owned two parcels on Elm Street in the 1810-1815 timeframe. One being on the west side of 'the green.' The other parcel appears to be on the corner of Main Street and Elm on the north side of the green. While none of the deeds refer to him being a whip maker or having a whip shop, these properties would be appropriate locations for what newspaper accounts attributing him as being a whip maker described.

Farnham left Westfield prior to 1820 when he was listed in the Federal Census as being in Tioga, New York. There were no registered deeds for Joel Farnham between 1818 and 1831. A final Westfield deed with Joel Farnham selling a single parcel listing his address as Mechanicville, New York was recorded in 1831. Joel died in 1831 in Mechanicsville, N.Y.

Franklin Arthur

Franklin Arthur appears to have started making whips as early as 1820 based on an article on Sept 6, 1873 from the *Commercial Bulletin* newspaper of Boston which stated:

> "- F. Arthur, of Westfield, Mass., claims to be the oldest whip maker in that town, and has been in the business 53 years. He commenced the manufacture of what was then called a first-class whip in 1820. This whip was made from white-oak timber, covered with sheep skin. Mr. Arthur is 76 years of age, but still works at the business."

Federal Census records of 1850, 1860 and 1870 all describe his occupation as farmer, as does the 1865 State Census. However, the Massachusetts State census of 1855 listed his occupation as a whip maker.

A newspaper article from the *Springfield Republican* describes a fire on Mar. 7, 1855, providing confirmation on his being a whip maker in the Little River section. (see chapter on fires for details).

A deed of 1849 describes Franklin Arthur having purchased that property from the estate of Samuel Arnold. The property described is 3 acres of land bordering the canal on the west, at what is now Little River Road & Tow Path Lane. The deed also states that the parcel is bounded on its south side by land he already owns (where his mother was living). Additionally, the *1855 Map of Hampden County* confirms two parcels noted as F. Arthur side by side on Little River road at the proper locations.

The property is currently the home of Dennis Picard, a well-known historian and former director of Storrowton Village at the Eastern States Exposition in West Springfield, Ma. Mr. Picard was aware of Arthur Franklin having formerly owned the house and the fact there had been a fire in 1855.

However, he wasn't aware Arthur Franklin was also one of the early whip makers of Westfield and had made whips on the property due to the lack of whip related details in any of the common publications, deeds or records from that time.

Courtesy Dennis Picard

While newspaper articles combined with the deeds and 1857 Atlas confirm Franklin Arthur as a whip maker and his location, there are likely many more Westfield farmers making whips who weren't fortunate or, in this case, unfortunate enough to experience events worthy of being reported in the newspapers giving us insight to their existence.

Edwin Phelps versus Salmon Phelps

A sketch of the Wyben community, located in the northwest corner of Westfield, written in 1935 by Edward Caldwell Jones, provides early documentation of a whip factory located there.

The sketch describes Edwin Phelps having operated a whip shop beginning in 1820 at what later became the Wyben Creamery. However, Edwin Phelps who died in 1889 at the age of 73, appears to have been too young. His father Salmon was born in 1785 and newspaper articles from the 1830's confirm his residing in Wyben near the town line on the road to Montgomery. Additionally, Salmon's death record of 1873 describes him as being a Whip Maker. These facts would appear to indicate it was Salmon who started the whip shop in the 1820's not Edwin.

Summary

While Joseph Joke's authenticity may be in question (at least to this author), Franklin Arthur, Titus Pease, Samuel Lindsay, Joel Farnum and Salmon Phelps are described in multiple sources and accounts as being both residents of Westfield and having been were involved in the manufacture of whips. At the very least, it is safe to assume these men were involved in the earliest stages of Westfield's whip industry.

The Whip Plaiting/Braiding Machine – Who was first ?

From the early 1800's until around 1820 the whips were described as being completely handmade. The introduction of whip plaiting (pronounced 'platting') machines for weaving the outer covering around the handles (stocks) began between 1810 and 1820.

Prior to the introduction of these machines, plaiting or braiding was a slow and tedious process and a typical day's work would be a dozen, four-foot whips or 48 feet. Using the machines, a normal days output was increased to 300 feet with some experienced workers achieving twice or more that amount.

Most historical accounts also describe the early 'plaiting machine' as being very primitive and amounted to little more than a barrel through which the whip stock was fed and the covering was 'plaited' (braided) around. The covering strands were held by weights as the braider worked his way around the barrel braiding the leather strips back and forth until the stock was fully covered. However, the first individual to introduce these machines has been debated for some time.

Joel Farnham (a.k.a. Farnum) has been credited by some with introducing plaiting machines in Westfield around 1810. Reportedly, D.L. Farnham was sent to Boston by his father (Joel). An article in the *Springfield Republican* on Mar. 26, 1865 repeated the story. The story claims that he arrived early at a whip shop before anybody had arrived for work and observed some braiding machines which had been kept secret from the outside world. He hastily drew diagrams of the devices which he brought back to Westfield where the machines were reproduced from these hand drawn pictures. While repeating the legend, the article has some inconsistencies in that it estimated the time as 1819 or 1820, while other accounts placed it closer to 1810.

Still another article, published in 1887 by the *Boston Herald*, gives credit for the first plaiting machine as having been copied from a Boston shop around 1817. This accounting gives credit to Samuel Lindsay who spirited away the details for the plaiting machine. The article goes on to credit Lindsay with developing many improvements beyond those normally credited to Farnham but it also has several inaccurate dates and details making the value of the report questionable.

Some accounts credit Hull for bringing the primitive machines to Westfield as early as 1810. However, Hull would have been 14 years old at that time making those accounts highly questionable.

The two Boston based accounts appear to describe the earlier and more primitive barrel-like devices. Also, both Boston accounts support the possibility that at least some of the earliest plaiting machines had their origins in Boston. Given that Lindsay and Farnham appear to have started whip shops around the same time (1810) in Westfield, it is possible that whichever one of the two actually obtained the design via Boston, he simply may have shared it with the other one. Given those facts, a case could be made that the accounts of Lindsay or Farnham introducing the simple barrel-like devices may be appropriate.

Hiram Hull and the Thorp patented braider/plaiting device

While it can be theorized that Farnham or Lindsey were the ones who introduced the primitive whip braider, Hiram Hull's obtaining the rights to the Thorp patent and bringing it to Westfield is arguably the one deserving credit for the first true whip braiding/plaiting machine. Hull is well documented as having bought the patent rights for a braiding machine from a Mr. Thorp of Providence, Rhode Island for $1500 in 1821.

The Thorp patent letters clearly describe a complex machine with components such as carriers with convex/concave surfaces, plates and shafts for the carriers to move around in circles, the use of bobbins and spools, etc. (A full transcription of the Thorp Patent application is included in the Appendices).

While, there aren't any diagrams of the Thorp machine available, the Halliday patent of 1838, illustrated in the Patents chapter, was described as an improvement to the Thorp machine. The diagram clearly a illustrates a more complex, engineered device with machined parts than would have been used on the more primitive barrel-like devices.

By some accounts, Hull obtained the full rights to the machines implying Thorp relinquished full control for his machines. However, later documents refute that assertion. An 1832 agreement between Hull and Martin Day stated that Day paid two hundred dollars for "the right of using and vending the same to be used in the town of Westfield." In that agreement, it was also stated that Hull's rights per the agreement with Thorp were:

> "conveyed to me all of his right and interest in the braiding machine aforesaid, so far as the said machine can be applied to the covering of whip stocks & for no other purposes whatever..."

The agreement also goes on to note that Hull's rights included both Thorpe's original patent and a patented improvement of 1826. Thus, Thorp only relinquished interest and control of his devices in regards to the whip industry not the full patent as some have reported.

As can be seen from the agreement with Martin Day, Hull benefitted in two ways from his acquisition of Thorp's patent. First, his own company prospered via the use of the machines in manufacturing whips. Second, Hull profited as a distributor, by virtue of being able to market the machines and license their use by other Westfield whip manufacturers. As reported in the *Westfield Standard*

Times, each machine cost $240.00 and by 1850 about 60 of these devices had been installed in different establishments in Westfield.

Early Whip Manufacturers - 1825-55

By 1825, the industry was evolving from the model of individual farmers producing whips into established shops most of which were located near the center of Westfield's downtown district.

Following the earlier whip makers already discussed, the next wave of early whip manufacturers included:

        Hiram Hull   Martin Day Jr.
        Hiram Harrison   David N. Day
        Jasper R. Rand   Samuel Dow
        James and Rueben Noble   Edward B. Gillett

In addition to migrating away from the farms and outlying shops. This next generation differed from the earlier whip makers in another way. While the earlier whip makers were often farmers and tradesmen, as the industry developed the new whip makers were businessmen and financial investors. Many were officers and directors of Westfield banks and almost without exception they had other investments and businesses such as cigar and other companies in Westfield.

A *Springfield Republican* article of October 8, 1851, illustrated this when it listed the officers of the banks of Hampden County. In Westfield, the directors of Hampden Bank included Hiram Hull, Samuel Dow, E.B. Gillett and James Noble. Directors of Westfield Bank included J.R. Rand and Hiram Harrison.

A subsequent article from the Springfield Republican in 1859 listed many of the same whip manufacturers amongst the directors of Hampden Cigar, one of Westfield's largest cigar manufacturers at that time. Included amongst the directors were Hiram Harrison, William Provin, E.B. Gillett, and L.R. Norton who was also the treasurer of the company.

Their financial standing in the banks and other Westfield businesses provided the access to the resources required to build their companies and become the power brokers of the industry during the 1850's and 60's. Meanwhile, Lindsey, Farnham, Phelps and many other small whip makers all faded from the scene within a few years.

The manufacture of whips becomes a major industry for Westfield and Hampden County.

By the early 1830's the rapid growth of Westfield's whip industry positioned it as a major player in Hampden County's economy. An article of Feb 15, 1832 in the *Hampden Whig* (Springfield, Mass.) included the following:

> "The following are aggregates from the *'Statistical view of the Arts and Industry of Hampden County.* Prepared with much labor by a committee appointed at the New York Tariff Convention for the purpose and recently published'."
> ………..
> "Firearms & c. [16,500]   187,500
> Paper, 49,324,reams [all by D. & J. Ames]   150,000
> Saddles, harnesses, whips & c. (of
> Whips alone in Westfield about
> $100,000) made, are valued at   121,882
> Leather manufactured   120,900
> Wool used,   115,525
> Boots and shoes   97,750
> Rags & C. for paper manufacturers,
> 1,568,167 lbs.   90,720
> Palm-leaf and straw hats, & c.   86,050"

By this account, in the relatively short span of 10 years since the Hull machines were introduced, the whip industry with its value of $100,000 in Westfield alone, had already become the 5th largest industry in Hampden County.

Another example of the ongoing growth and its impact on Westfield was noted by an entry in the *Massachusetts Directory* of 1835. The entry for Westfield included the following statement.

> "About a third of its population is engaged in making whips. The annual amount of that article manufactured here is about $150,000."

The claim than one third of its population was involved with making whips appears inflated. Regardless, it affirmed the whip industry's position as a dominate influence on Westfield's economy.

The 1840 US Census combined with a *Springfield Republican* article on Jan. 13, 1838 provided a more accurate assessment. The newspaper article summarized whip statistics for Westfield as follows;

        Whip Manufactories – 13
        Value of Manufactured Whips - $153,000
        Males Employed – 154
        Females Employed – 410

With the 1840 U.S. Census recording Westfield's population at 3526, the above figures from 1838 claiming 564 persons were employed in the whip industry accounts for approximately 16% of the overall population. Factoring in children, the elderly, et al. a more plausible statement is possibly that one third or more of the available workforce was engaged in making whips.

As the industry grew, Westfield's position as a leader in the industry is evidenced by the number of articles which began appearing in newspapers across the country. Whip related newspaper postings of almost any nature were regularly forwarded and reported in Boston, New York, Connecticut and many other states across the country. A small sampling of typical articles posted elsewhere:

<u>Jun. 24, 1833</u>, *Courier*, Charleston, S.C. (a repost from the Springfield Journal)
> "…..The two principle factories at Westfield belong to Martin Day and Hiram Hull; and we presume that at these two factories more than $100,00 worth of the article of every price and variety is annually made; and the demand for the work is more than equal to the manufacture…"

<u>Apr. 1, 1836,</u> *The Recorder*, Boston, Ma.
> " The town of Westfield in this state, is probably without a rival in the whip manufacture. Five or six extensive establishments in that town turn out Whips annually to the amount of $500,000…"

> The same article was published in the *North Carolina Standard*, of Raleigh N.C. on April 4, 1836.

<u>May 10, 1838,</u> *American and Commercial Advertiser*, Baltimore, Md.
> "A Curious Robbery! – The Whip factory of J.R. Rand & Co. in Westfield, Mass. was broken open and Whips and lashes to the amount of $2000 stolen….."

July 24, 1846, *Rochester Democrat*, Rochester, N.Y. (as reposted in the Springfield Republican).
"Taylor's Whip Factory, Observing the sign of a whip factory elevated to the third story of the building near our office"......, (the article continues) ......"Westfield Mass contains 12 whip factories. Some of the workmen here are from that town, but a days work by a female in Mr. Taylor's factory, last week, they considered a stump even for Westfield."

Modernization and its impact on the Westfield whip makers

The introduction of the original Thorp braiding machines by Hiram Hull in 1822 jump started the modernization and industrialization of the industry which would continue throughout the century. While modernization vastly improved the ability to manufacture a high volume of quality whips, over the long term, it created a widening gap between the 'haves' and the 'have nots' amongst the whip companies. As time went on, production of completely handmade whips decreased as whip factories utilizing braiding/plaiting and other machines increased. The larger firms having the financial resources, built factories capable of covering the full range of machinery needed for a complete manufactory. For those whip makers not fortunate enough to have the financial resources required for a complete manufactory, there were several choices for survival.

* One option was to pool their resources (e.g. merge into new companies) enabling them to obtain the full range of equipment they required.
* A second option would be to focus on specific manufacturing roles needing only a limited number or specific type of machine such as making/turning stocks, mountings/holders, buttons.
* Another was to continue producing articles which didn't require the newer machines such as manufacturing lashes or snaps by hand or specialty items such as toys whips and other accessories.

Several of the smaller whip makers chose the second or third options of specialization making solely stocks, lashes or other parts of the whip, effectively becoming 'jobbers' for the larger firms.

Of the men who chose the path of specialization, several had very successful companies lasting 15 or more years. The following table lists some of the longer running operations.

Specialty	Name	Years	Duration in years
Lashes	Horace Avery & Family	1872 – 1939	68
	Jay M. Barnes	1870 – 1897	28
	Enoch Phelps	1879 – 1898	20
	George Sackett	1860 – 1878	19
	Lester Loomis	1855 – 1878	24
	Lemuel Grant	1874 – 1889	16
Stocks	Charles Hadley	1872 – 1893	22
	J.J. Bohler	1865 – 1894	29
	Dibble & Randall	1872 – 1886	15
Buttons	Palmer & Upson	1896 – 1915	20
Machinery	C.A. Hastings	1892 – 1911	20
	M. E. Moore (& son)	1883 – 1914	31
Mountings	James Whipple (& son)	1867 – 1896	29
Plaiting/Machines	Emerson Sizer	1856 – 1879	24
Plaiting/ Coverings	George T. Moore	1874 – 1918	34
	Westfield Plaiting Co.	1882 – 1897	16
Holly Whips	L.R. Sweatland	1891 – 1910	20
Toy Whips	A.D. Fuller	1879 – 1896	18
Toy & Riding Whips	Chas. Douglas & Co.	1873 – 1889	17

There were a large number of individuals and companies who chose the partnership/merger path. However, while the whip industry continued to grow rapidly, it was also a very volatile environment to survive in. Many companies existed for just a year or two before dissolving or merging with other partners, only to once again separate.

Regardless of which of the paths they chose to take, less than 25 per cent of the companies in this era existed under a single name or operation for 10 years or more.

During the early years, the whip men and companies were often listed simply as whip manufacturers. Over time, as the industry matured, the description of the firms in city directories, State and Federal Census records, and various other state and local reports became more descriptive.

Descriptions such as: manufacturers of whips, buttons, stocks, lashes, machinery, plaiting/coverings, mounts, etc. became more common. These details allowed for a better understanding of each firm. These descriptions also help identify which of the firms were the full manufacturers versus the 'jobbers' or sub-contractors supplying parts to the major concerns.

One of the first formal records illustrating how the companies were specializing was the 1850 Federal Census's Special Manufacturing Schedule. This schedule provided statistics on company names, numbers of employees, wages, type of business and value of goods produced.

Sixteen companies were identified as whip makers. Three made whip lashes only and one made Whip mountings.

A Summary from the 1850 Census Report:

Company / Individual	Employees	Quantities	Value $
Lashes			
A. G. Chadwick	4 male 20 female	12,000 doz.	6,500
Ezra Hubbard	2 male 50 female	16,000 doz.	8,000
Solomon Shepard	1 male	1,200 doz.	1,000
Mountings			
Dudley D. Sacket	6 males 1 female	2400 doz.	3,000
Whips (and lashes)			
Dow, Loomis & Co.	20 male 56 females	2,000 doz. whips	25,000
John Loomis	6 male 10 females	750 doz. whips	8,000
L. W. Lewis	7 male 4 females	1200 doz. whips	7,500
Gross, Jonah L. & Co.	16 male 40 females	2,000 doz. whips 3,000 doz. thong	20,000

Company / Individual	Employees	Quantities	Value $
Hiram Hull	9 male 15 females	2,000 doz. whips	12,000
James Noble (1)	10 males 25 females	2,000 doz. whips 4,000 doz. lashes	18,000
Hiram Harrison (1)	40 males 75 females	6,000 doz. whips 12,000 doz. lashes	44,800
Lyman H. Lewis	4 males 6 females	800 doz. whips	5,000
Loomis & ?? (2)	4 males	1,200 doz. whips	6,000
James Miller	2 males 6 females	800 doz. whips	5,000
John Shepard & Co.	2 males	1,200 doz. whips	3,000
Jasper R. Rand	12 males 20 females	3,000 doz. whips 10,000 doz. lashes	20,000
A. R. Van Deusen	12 males 21 females	4,320 doz. whips	25,000
Junior B. Smith	2 males	300 doz. whips	1,500
Munroe & Brownson	10 males 8 females	1,404 doz. whips	11,500
William Provin	6 males 1 female	1,000 doz. whips	9,000
Totals	131 males 357 females		$ 213,000

By the above accounting, the statistics gathered totaled an annual production over almost 350,000 whips and an additional 680,000 thongs and lashes.

Notes:
(1) Both James Noble and Hiram Harrison also produced cigars which were accounted for separately.
(2) Although not listed as whip related, two men Alexander McNeil and Daniel Smith had tanneries with a combined product value of almost $3000. It's probable that a significant portion of their goods were sold to the whip makers.

The volatility of the whip industry is exhibited by the fact that only three companies shown on the 1850 Census report continued to operate into the 1860's under their original names. These were the firms of William Provin, Jasper R. Rand and A.R. Van Deusen

William Provin and Co., founded in 1849, would not only survive into the next decade, it would operate continually until 1902. By that time, William Provin would become the longest running whip company in the industry having operated for 53 years.

Jasper Rand & Co. After Jasper R. Rand passed away in 1869, his sons continued operating the company until Feb. 1870 by which time it was Rand, Lewis & Rand when it was purchased by American Whip. Jasper's surviving sons left Westfield for New York City by 1871, subsequently forming Rand Rock Drill Company in New Jersey. Rand Rock Drill Co. eventually merged with the Ingersoll-Sargent Drill Company becoming the Ingersol-Rand Corporation. Although the Rand brothers relocated to New York and later New Jersey, the Rand family retained a strong presence in Westfield. Jasper R. Rand and his sons are all buried in Westfield's Pine Hill Cemetery with many of their family members. The Rand family also became benefactors of the Westfield Athenaeum with the Jasper Rand Art Museum named after the patriarch of the family.

Alonzo R. Van Deusen would operate until 1868 when it was merged into American Whip with Alonzo and Merritt Van Deusen becoming major investors in the company and soon thereafter officers.

Three of the listed companies became the foundation of American Whip Co. The firms of Hiram Harrison, Hiram Hull and Samuel Dow (Dow & Loomis) who were among the longest running Westfield whip companies merged in 1855 establishing American Whip Company. The merger was arguably the most significant merger in the history of the whip industry until the creation of United States Whip Co. in 1892. Based on the statistics of 1850 (which would have grown significantly by 1855) the combination of these firms would have accounted for the employment of at last 215 people (70 males/145 female) and production of 120,000 whips and 144,000 lashes per year.

It is also known there were many more individuals making small quantities of whips on farms or in their own small shops who were not accounted for in these schedules. The Phelps family of Wyben being one example. As noted previously, the 1935 *Sketch of Wyben* by Edward Caldwell Jones, provides background documentation on a Phelps' whip factory located there. However, neither Salmon or Edwin Phelps, who are both documented whip makers, were included in the 1850 Census Manufacturing Schedule. Likewise, Arthur Franklin, of the Little River section of town, who was primarily a farmer and an acknowledged whip maker, was not included in these statistics.

Another 'hidden' statistic is the number of people employed in their homes braiding lashes & snaps. An article printed in the *Westfield Standard* on Aug. 1851 appears to have included both the 'in-shop' and out of shop" employees for some of the larger firms. In that accounting, the newspaper listed both males and females, with an additional notation for the number of 'braiders', with the implication that the braiders were people braiding outside of the shop.

Company	Total Males & Females	Braiders
E. R. Van Deusen	18	25
J.L. Gross & Co.	27	30
H. Hull & Son	15	100
J.R. Rand	20-25	40-50
Monroe & Bronson	8	
W. S. Provin	9	20-25
Dow & Loomis & Co.	60	50
H. Harrison & Co.	54	A large number

While this list is only a sampling of the larger companies, it provided insight to the high number of people engaged with braiding lashes outside of the shops and the difficulty in being able to truly understand the full extent of how much of the population was engaged in the whip industry.

The column for Total Males & Females is in-line with the 1850 census, however as noted previously, the census failed to account for the braiders.

Middle Era (1855 - 1893)

Whips become a dominant industry

The era from 1855 until 1893 was not only the period of significant growth, it was also a time of major innovation and invention on the part of Westfield whip makers. In addition to the raw numbers of whips produced, Westfield's improvements of whip making techniques, materials and the machines employed were all driving factors to Westfield's establishing and maintaining its dominance in the industry.

Between 1855 and 1893, Westfield had over 130 Patents for inventions attributable to its whip makers. Of those patents, 30 were specifically noted as inventions or improvements to the machines. The remaining 100 plus patents applied to improved materials, braiding methods, and various other improvements to whip construction. Within the patents applying to improved whip construction, there were often references to adjustments or improvements to the machines, making the number of machine related innovations even greater than the patents specifically classified as machine related.

During this time there were several individuals who specialized in both making whip machines and selling them both within Westfield and to companies located elsewhere.

By 1855, the whip industry had grown to be the pre-eminent manufacturing industry in Westfield. The State of Massachusetts publication, *Statistics of Massachusetts Industry* summarized Westfield industries as follows:

	Value of produced goods	Employees
Whip factories (number not specified)	$ 420,000	263
Factories for Snuff, tobacco and cigars (number not specified)	$ 49,900	62
1 Paper Factory	$ 75,000	40
1 Organ Factory	$ 30,000	25
2 Powder Mills	$ 24,000	7

3 Box factories: 1 Cigar, 1 whip, 1 fancy boxes	$ 20,000	7
2 establishments for manufacturing steam engines and boilers	$ 15,000	13
1 Furnace for manufacturing of hollow ware and castings	$ 10,000	8
3 Flour Mills	$ 10,000	5
1 Cotton Mill	$ 7,700	8
2 Tanneries	$ 6,000	4
Firewood Prepared for Market	$ 4,012	20
2 Tin Ware factories	$ 4,000	7
1 Brick factory	$ 4,000	12
Lumber prepared for Market	$ 3,500	5
2 Chair and Cabinet factories	$ 3,000	4
2 factories for the manufacture of railroad cars, coaches, chaises, wagons, sleighs, etc.	$ 2,500	4
2 Saddle, Harness and Trunk Factories	$ 2,000	6
Boots & Shoes	$ 1,900	9
Quarried Stone	$ 500	4

Miscellaneous Westfield statistics from agricultural and non-industry related categories included:

	Value
Livestock, including Horses, Oxen, Sheep, Cows and Cattle	$ 70,643
Multiple styles of Corn, Wheat, Rye and general field grown crops including tobacco	$ 52, 182
Butter, Cheese & Honey	$ 13,496
Vegetables and fruit	$ 6,808
Hay, 2,614 tons of English Hay were harvested from 1,733 acres accounting for $41,824, the remainder was 310 tons of Wet Meadow or Swale Hay	$ 43,684

In the preceding tables, the whip industry value was $420,000 with all other industrial and agricultural values totaling $459,000. As such, according to these state reports, the whip industry was 48% of Westfield's overall economy, clearly establishing its importance to the town.

A second accounting from the state of Massachusetts in 1855 focused on the prominent industries in towns and cities across the commonwealth. That report which summarized statistics by counties listed the whip statistics as follows:

	WHIPS	
	Value of whips manufactured	Hands Employed
Berkshire	12,000	39
Franklin	700	2
Hampden	412,400	268
Hamsphire	3,050	6
Middlesex	61,400	44
Norfolk	950	4
Suffolk	3,000	2
Worcester	3,000	2
Totals	505,000	367

* The counties of Barnstable, Bristol, Dukes, Essex and Plymouth reported no whip industry.

Details within the document further highlight Westfield dominance.

- The Middlesex county figures represent whip manufacturing in the Charlestown State Prison which was done under a contract with American Whip of Westfield. (Charlestown was later switched to Suffolk county in 1874.)
- The Berkshire county values are from shops manufacturing primarily whip lashes versus full whips.
- The Hamsphire county numbers are from the town of Southampton which borders Westfield.

Combining the Suffolk County figures, which are actually American Whip Co.'s with the Hampden county statistics, establishes Westfield's whip industry as accounting for 94% of the value of whips produced and employing 85% of the people working in the whip industry for the commonwealth, once again confirming Westfield as the hub of the whip industry in Massachusetts.

While the size of the whip industry in Westfield clearly reflects the dominance of whip manufacturing in relation to the remainder of the state, the number of people reported in this accounting is significantly lower than was reported locally and in other reports issued by the state.

Historians and various other accounts gave the following accounting of whip companies in Westfield for 1855.

> Dow & Gillett, whips & whip thongs, 100 hands
> J & R Noble, whips. lashes & cigars, 100 hands
> Wm. Provin & Co., whips, 100 hands
> H. Harrison & Co., whips, 300 hands
> J.R. Rand & Co., whips, harnesses, thongs, etc., 50 hands in shop, 20 out
> King & Avery, whips, 10 hands

These figures would have put the number of persons employed in the whip industry at over 600 hands, significantly greater than the state statistics.

It is important to note that while the accountings by various historians highlighted many of the major firms, there was never a full accounting of the industry. Additionally, the statistics for the number of people employed, number of whips and their overall value were likely inflated in some accounts, as they were used for advertisements, trade shows and other publications where the numbers tended to be reported higher to enhance a company's status.

Whip statistics which had been compiled for the Western Hampden Agricultural Show and Fair in Oct. 1860 illustrate the dominance of American Whip over the other whip manufacturers in Westfield. Based on the values reported, American Whip produced over 62% of the total value of whips manufactured and accounted for 55-60% of the hands employed.

Selected statistics from the account pertinent to the Whip industry include:

Company	Value of Whips Manufactured	Hands Employed
American Whip Company	$350,000	300
Jasper R. Rand	80,000	75-100
Lester Holcomb	50,000	58
James P. Whipple	2,500	6

Gillett, Spencer and Co.	25,000	20
William Provin	15,000	15
Shepard, Holcomb and Cook	20,000	20
Edward Swan	8,000	12
Henry Mygatt	7,000	10
Totals	**557,500**	**516-541**

The summary from the Agricultural Show statistics further highlights the wide variance in figures reported from different sources. The values given here would have indicated a 35% growth of goods produced and a nearly 100% growth in the people employed in a mere 5 years when compared to the census figures.

However, another explanation is that the variances illustrate the inconsistent nature of the industry. In the 1800's the industry went through several periods of strong growth, soon to be followed by stagnant business activity when factories would reduce to part time work or even shut down completely for brief periods. As such, individual reports compiled during prosperous times versus lean times yielded very different results.

1860 US Federal Census – Manufacturing Schedule, accumulated statistics

In 1860, the government once again included special schedules for both agriculture and manufacturing, supplementing the general population schedules. Similar to the 1850 census, these schedules attempted to compile a full accounting for the respective statistics for each town. However, once again, the census statistics don't fully account for the number of people employed in Westfield's whip industry as once again it didn't include women braiding at home or individuals known to have been making items such whip stocks and other smaller articles which they then sold to the firms.

However, the Manufacturing Schedules provide insight into several items of interest that other reports often do not include.

According to this schedule there were nineteen whip manufactures in Westfield, employing 384 males and 302 females with an annual value of products produced equaling $514,200. There were five manufacturers listed as specifically making lashes employing another 10 males and 51 females with a total value of $23,500. When combined, these two statistics equate to total of 747 hands employed and a total value of goods produced at $537,700.

In comparison, Westfield's next largest industry was the manufacturing of cigars. In 1860 there were a total of 9 firms employing 224 hands, making 12 Million cigars with a value of $245,700.

The continuing disparity in pay between males and females is another statistic worthy of mention. As with many industries, the issue was both widespread and consistent across the manufacturers. Wages for males in the whip companies was consistently $30 - $40 a month, while females were only compensated $12 a month. The Cigar industry exhibited a very similar gap in male versus female compensation.

The statistics for the method of 'Motive Power' for machinery makes it clear that the whip companies were just beginning to incorporate steam and water power for their factories. Of the nineteen whip manufacturers, only two (Gamaliel King and American Whip) used steam power. Three of the companies (Jasper Rand, James Whipple and Edwin Phelps of West Farms/Wyben) employed water power. Lester Holcomb's shop rounded out the six, reporting a combination of water and hand power. The remaining thirteen still used hand power.

Jasper Rand's whip shop being water powered would likely come as a surprise to many today. The factory was located on Elm Street across from Franklin Street on what was later the site of the Textile Manufacturing/Power Company Building. In today's world, this location has no apparent source of water to power a factory.

The following image showing, a small section of downtown Westfield, is an extract from the *1857 Atlas of Hampden County*. The dark arrow is pointing to the J.R. Rand Factory on Elm Street across from Franklin Street. The map shows where the stream starts at the bottom of the image, flows north crossing Franklin Street, then turns east crossing Elm Street and then Mechanic Street. The stream is no longer visible due to its running underground.

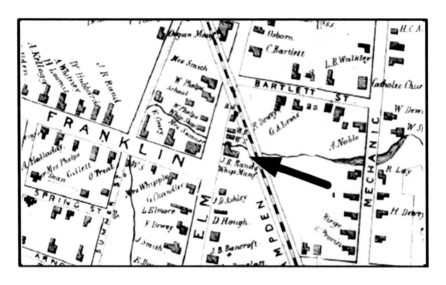

Extract from *Map of Hampden County, 1857*

American Whip Company, establishment of a dynasty

In May of 1855, the first and most important merger of whip manufacturers was the formation of American Whip. At that time, three of the largest firms in Westfield were those of Hiram Hull, Hiram Harrison and that of E.B. Gillett & Samuel Dow. Hull, Harrison and Dow combined to form the American Whip Company. It appears that E.B. Gillett left the group at that time, or shortly thereafter, as he was listed as part of Gillett, Spencer & Co. in 1860.

As stated previously, the merger creating American Whip is arguably the single most important merger in the industry's early history. American Whip would go on to become the largest, longest surviving and most powerful whip company during the halcyon years of the industry. American Whip also became the nucleus of the 1892 merger of many of the whip companies, creating the United States Whip Corporation.

Another distinction of American Whip which differentiated it from the other firms is that it broke the mold of single or limited ownership of a company. Historically the whip companies where run by just one or two men under their own names, while American Whip was truly a modern corporation.

Also, within a few years, Hiram Hull, Sam Dow and Hiram Harrison had all departed from American Whip leaving the corporation in the hands of a board of directors and professional whip manufacturers versus private owners. In 1861, Sam Dow would exit the whip business, becoming Westfield pre-eminent florist/horticulturalist. The year 1861 also saw the passing of Hiram Hull. Hiram Harrison became the last to depart when he resigned the presidency in 1865 due to ill health. With the assumption of the presidency by Henry J. Bush and the establishment of a new slate of officers, American Whip entered a new era of corporate management.

New companies, partnerships, mergers and dissolutions.

During the second half of the 19th century the most common estimate of whip companies in Westfield is usually in the range of 30 to 40 companies at any given point in time.

However, over 300 names of people/shops described as whip manufacturers can be extracted from the various sources of information available for the second half of the century. This does not include people described simply as whip makers who were working as employees of the manufacturers.

One indication of the ongoing volatility of the industry can be seen by the number of companies which existed for only a year or two before changing names or vanishing from existence, even during the periods of high growth in the industry. Less than 30% of the companies existed for 10 years or more.

There were only six whip manufacturers formed prior to 1870 which continued to operate into the 1890's.

        These were: American Whip
                                     Derrick N. Goff
                                     Gamaliel King
                                     Joseph King (& son)
                                     Jay M. Barnes
                                     William Provin

While the whip industry continued to grow in the second half of the century, it continued to be a very unpredictable business. Increasing competition, rising prices, and an unsteady economy all contributed to the challenges of being able to sustain an ongoing successful business. The volatility of the industry and frequent name changes created challenges with documenting and tracking the existence of the various whip shops, their partnerships and the length of time they operated.

An example of the volatility of the whip industry is the following example of how four whip companies would evolve into twelve different firms in less than ten years. The chart following the narrative shows the firms as noted.

The four initial companies in the example: (1) E.B. Light Co., (2) Pratt, Atwater & Co., (3) Osden Brothers Whip Co. and (4) George S. Peck all existed prior to 1872.

The first change in 1873 involved E.L. Goodnow joining (2) Pratt, Atwater & Co. establishing (5) Pratt, Atwater & Goodnow. That relationship lasted less than one year when Goodnow departed and William H. Owen joined the firm, resulting in a name change to (6) Pratt, Atwater & Owen. When the company went bankrupt in 1874, Leonard Atwater purchased his former company's equipment at auction and established (7) Hampden Whip with previous partners C.C. Pratt and E.L. Goodnow. Soon after Hampden's establishment, (1) E.B. Light was absorbed in the new company. Hampden Whip would eventually be bought out by American Whip in 1883.

After Pratt, Atwater & Owen when bankrupt, William H. Owen partnered with the Osden Brothers (3) forming (8) Owen, Osden & Co in 1876. That relationship was short lived with William Owen and the Osdens parting company after less than 2 years. William H. Owen then formed a company in his own name (9).

With the departure of William H. Owen, the Osden brothers would next establish a partnership with George S. Peck as (10) Peck & Osden. However, this relationship would be dissolved in 1881 after just three years. Next, the Osden brothers next established (11) Osden Whip Company and Peck re-established (12) George S. Peck Whip Co.

This example illustrates some of the challenges with documenting the whip companies due to the changing partners. It also illustrates how the longevity of some companies can be misconstrued. Without understanding the details, one could conclude incorrectly that George S. Peck operated his firm continuously for a longer period than actually true. Likewise, the Osden brothers did not operate their company continuously for over 20 years as might have been thought if the intervening companies weren't understood.

Additionally, while the chart doesn't illustrate it, the name changes were as often due to financial relationships as opposed to the working partner relationships of the whip makers themselves. Neither E.L. Goodnow or William H. Owen were actual whip makers, they were financial men and their involvement was as investors. Additionally, while Leonard Atwater was known as an early whip maker, he likewise was primarily a business man by this time.

The Osdens, C.C. Pratt, E.B. Light and George S. Peck were the true whip makers of this group. Lonzene Osden (1), C.C. Pratt (6) and E.B. Light (2) all also held whip patents.

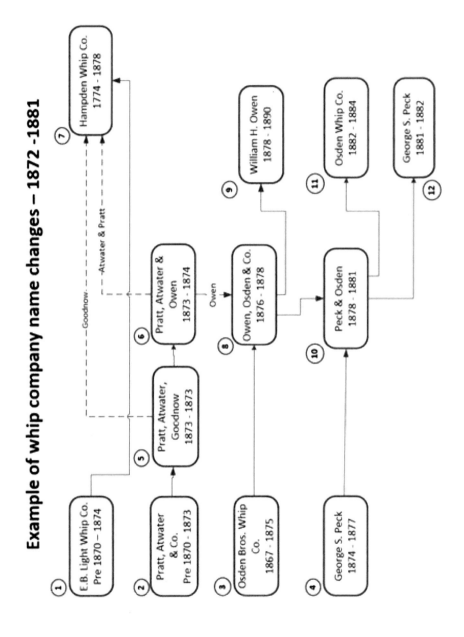

Another factor affecting the whip shops were multiple periods of a slow or depressed economy affecting the entire country and the whip industry was no more prone to escaping those affects than any other industry. Reports of significant growth soon followed by periods of stagnate activity were common. It was not uncommon to see reports of shops working full time or overtime during surges in business activity then shortly thereafter cutting back to half time or even shutting down briefly when business lagged. These cycles of high activity to low or no activity would occur throughout the second half of the century.

The unpredictability of the whip industry was not isolated to Westfield. An article in the *Commercial Advertiser* of New York City on July 3, 1846, reposted a report from the *Rochester Democrat* describing the three major whip concerns of Rochester. The companies of William R. Strong, Isaac Taylor, and Gerry, McMaster & Burnett were described as employing a total of 30 to 50 men and boys and 125 females. However, by the time the 1850 Federal Census was compiled only Myron (son of William) Strong was listed. No further mention of the other 2 firms was noted. Additionally, the *History of Rochester* fails to mention either of the latter firms.

The Strong family is widely documented for having established their whip company in Rochester. Myron Strong's company similar to the Westfield firms would change ownership several times as it would become Strong and Woodbury Whip Co. and ultimately Woodbury Whip. Woodbury Whip in turn would be another Westfield acquisition when it was purchased by New England Whip in 1907.

Even with the erratic nature of the business, the whip industry continued to grow with the 1873 Westfield City Directory stating:

> "From a very small beginning this has grown to immense proportions. There are now some thirty-six whip factories, giving employment to 500 hands, with a capital of about $500,000, with sales amounting to nearly a million and a half of dollars per annum. These whips are of all styles grades and prices, from a children's toy whip to the finest quality of driving whip, which find their way to every city, village and hamlet in the union."

Interaction with other locations

Several Westfield men are known to have left Westfield to become involved with firms outside of Westfield throughout the middle to late 1800's, with many of those men returning to Westfield after a few years.

Also, as Westfield's whip industry grew, the involvement of whip companies from other areas of the country became more and more apparent. Newspaper articles of the 1860's and 70's increasingly mentioned those whip concerns and their involvement with the Westfield companies.

Rochester, N.Y.

One of the earliest Westfield whip men to leave the area was Frederick Morand. In his biography, *A Long and Busy Life* published in 1912, he wrote of having left Westfield to work in a Rochester firm for a couple years as a young man. He described meeting with Theron Ives who was leaving the area to establish a cheap whip factory in Rochester, N.Y.

Morand also named several other men as having left Westfield and going to Rochester to work in the Whip industry. They included: Henry Copley, Sanford Fuller, Gilbert King and Linus Noble. None of these men, including Frederick Morand, would remain in Rochester for more than a few years before leaving, returning to Westfield or going on to other careers.

Theron Ives, a sawmill owner from Russell left the Westfield area shortly after 1840, moving to Rochester. The Rochester City Directory of 1847-48 lists the whip shop of King & Ives at 31 Adams Street. The same address was also listed as Ives' residence with Gilbert King as boarding there. The 1849-50 directory listed the company as Ives & Co. Theron Ives' whip career and business in Rochester was over by 1860 when the Federal Census listed the Ives family as residing in Missouri with Theron's occupation reverting once again to that of a miller.

Gilbert King appears to be the brother of Mary Ann Ives (wife of Theron) whose maiden name was King. Gilbert and Mary Ann were also the siblings of Joseph King who would also become a well-known Westfield whip maker.

Sanford Fuller is confirmed as residing in Rochester as a whip maker via listings in the city directories, the US Federal Census of 1850 and the 1855 New York State Census. Sanford Fuller relocated to Ada, Michigan before 1860, where he was again listed as a whip maker in the 1860 Federal Census.

Linus (Linneas) Noble was born in Michigan but married Mary Fowler of Westfield. As with the others, Linneas is confirmed as being in Rochester in 1847 in the city directory listings. Additionally, per the 1850 Federal Census their daughter Augusta, born in 1846, was listed as having been born in the state of New York. That census also indicated the family had already relocated to Ada Michigan and Linneas had changed his occupation to ship builder.

Whether Henry Copley was in Rochester in the mid 1840's as a whip maker is unclear. However, Henry was back in Westfield by 1850 when he was listed as a whip maker, aged twenty-seven in the federal census. According to the same census Henry also would have returned by 1848, as the same census shows his son Jasper being 2 years old and born in Massachusetts.

Frederick Morand's biography also stated that Ives' shop was in the same building as the Strong Whip company. The 1851 Rochester directory lists both the Strong and Ives shops at 78 State Street confirming Morand's statement. Presumably, Ives either merged with Strong or more likely sold his shop prior to relocating to Missouri.

After returning to Westfield, Frederick Morand successfully embarked on a long and varied business career and would pass away in Westfield in 1913 as one of Westfield's wealthiest men.

Another Rochester N.Y. connection was Edward B. Light who established his whip shop in Westfield by 1870. E.B. Light was a native of Perinton, N.Y., a suburb of Rochester, where he was born in 1842.

The Westfield to Rochester connection continued when Lonzene M. Osden left Westfield in 1884 to join Strong and Woodbury in Rochester, New York. A May 13, 1886 newspaper article described a visit home.

> "L.M. Osden, formerly a local whip-manufacturer and now superintendent of a large whip factory at Rochester, N.Y. has been spending a few days at his old home calling on his numerous friends and looking after skilled workmen to increase the producing capacity of his factory."

Lonzene M. Osden, like many before him, would return to Westfield. By 1888, he had joined American Whip and was listed as a director of the company.

Windsor, New York

Windsor, New York, a small village near Binghampton, was the location for numerous whip shops from 1854 until the 1920's. Similar to Westfield, the whip industry was a significant industry to the little village. Arguably, it also had as many connections to Westfield men as Rochester or any of the other whip producing towns and cities.

When Adin Coburn, a shoemaker of Windsor N.Y., founded Coburn Whip in 1854, he recruited Rufus Morey a young whip maker from Westfield to move to Windsor N.Y. to help build the company. Rufus Morey is confirmed as being in Windsor by 1858 by virtue of the fact his son Edgar, was listed in the 1860 federal census as 2 years old and having been born in New York. Rufus Morey would remain in Windsor until the mergers with United States Whip in 1893.

Another link to the Westfield whip industry is shown in the 1880 Federal Census where Rufus Morey is listed next to Charles Comstock in order of visitation, indicating he was either next door or close by Comstock who was listed as a whip shop foreman. Comstock was at that time a foreman for Ira Owen. Two of Charles Comstock's sons, Edward and David would later relocate to Westfield to work for United States Whip with both ultimately serving terms as president of the company.

The volume, *Historical Essays of Windsor* by Marjory B. Hinman, published in 1976, documents the whip industry of Windsor, N.Y. in detail with excellent citations and sources. In that work, she includes Rufus Morey as documented previously. She also lists four other Westfield men as having been brought to Windsor in the 1874 timeframe. Those men were Albert Furrows and Charles Cowles to work for Coburn Whip, and W.H. Furrows and Henry Stiles working for the Owen Whip company. The publication goes on to state that at least 5 other Westfield men were counted in the 1875 New York census as working in the Windsor whip shops.

To date, Albert and Winslow H. Furrows and Ezra and Charles Cowles (two sets of brothers) have been verified as having been from Westfield and leaving the area relocating to Windsor as documented by Ms. Hinman. Henry Stiles has not been verified using census and local resources but given the depth to which Ms. Hinman documents her research, there is no reason to doubt her accuracy.

Another of Windsor's native sons, Edwin L. Sanford began his career in the Coburn whip shop in Windsor before joining American Whip Co. as a salesman. After a partnership in New York City in the firm Owen, Sanford & Co., he relocated to Westfield where he established Sanford Whip Co. in 1880.

While Windsor lost its two major whip shops to acquisitions by United States Whip, the village would continue to have independent whip shops until approximately 1950 when the last shop, Windsor Whip closed and the machinery was sold to a Westfield Whip factory. (Presumably, Harold Martin and Westfield Whip Manufacturing company.)

Hudson, Michigan

The Darling, Smith & Co. manufactory was in Westfield, but its business office was in Hudson, Michigan. A newspaper article of Oct. 4, 1871, gave an account of Charles W. Darling, a native of Leyden successfully running the Whip company in Hudson and the fact three of Charles' brothers worked in Darling & Smith or Westfield Whip. Both Westfield and Hudson, Mich. had multiple Darling families residing in their locales. Darling Smith & Co. and Westfield Whip Co merged in 1872. By 1873, C.W. Darling was listed in the Westfield City directories as boarding on N. Elm Street and working for Westfield Whip.

San Francisco, Ca.

In 1881, David Atwater left Westfield to establish his own whip company in San Francisco. Atwater established a successful business there before the San Francisco earthquake/fire disaster of 1906 destroyed both his business and home.

Social Affairs and Events

Coinciding with their annual meetings, the Whip Makers hosted major social events each year. On Aug. 2, 1854, Westfield's *Times Newsletter* described one of the earliest affairs as having been attended by three hundred sixty-nine people, including invited guests.

The account described the affair with Hiram Hull presiding, assisted by Hiram Harrison, Samuel Dow, James Noble and Jasper Rand. Per the article, the public supper was held at Blossom's Hotel.

The festivities became on a more formal event with the establishment of the First Annual Whip Makers Concert and Ball on Apr. 8, 1864, held at the Whitman Hall in the Whitman Block located at the corner of Elm and Church Streets. Tickets to just the concert were 25 cents and entry to both the concert and ball were $1.25.

The ball and concert became an annual social event for over 20 years, coinciding with the whip manufacturers meeting each year.

> # WHIP MAKERS'
> ## PROMENADE
> # Concert and Ball.
>
> The Whip Makers of Westfield,
> WILL GIVE THEIR
> # FIRST CONCERT AND BALL,
> ON
> ### WEDNESDAY EVENING, APRIL 6, 1864,
> AT
> ## WHITMAN HALL,
>
> *To which your Company with Ladies is respectfully solicited.*
>
> ---
>
> **Committee of Arrangements.**
>
> | | | |
> |---|---|---|
> | WILLIAM F. WHIPPLE, | CHARLES WHIPPLE, | BENNETT WEATHERBEE, |
> | S. W. KNIGHT, | NELSON HAYES, | H. B. STILES, |
> | D. S. COOLEY, | H. A. COWLES, | T. M. GRISWOLD, |
> | J. T. SMITH, | ALBERT FURROW, | J. B. FULLER, |
> | J. R. RAND, JR., | JAMES HAMILTON, | W. COWLES, |
> | V. O. COOLEY, | J. H. MONROE, | WILLIAM H. FURROW, |
> | H. HERRICK, | D. M. ATWATER, | L. S. DICKINSON, |
> | | L. O. JUDSON, | GEORGE WITT. |
>
> **Floor Managers.**
>
> | | | | |
> |---|---|---|---|
> | S. W. KNIGHT, | WM. F. WHIPPLE, | BENNETT WEATHERBEE, | V. O. COOLEY, |
> | J. H. MONROE, | T. M. GRISWOLD, | H. B. STILES, | L. O. JUDSON. |
>
> *MUSIC BY THE*
> # Germania Band, of Boston,
> A. HEINCHE, Leader.   J. H. WHITE, Prompter.
>
> **Tickets to Concert and Ball, $1.50. . . . Tickets to Concert, 25 Cents.**
>
> SUPPER AT THE WORONOCO HOUSE.
>
> Concert from 8 o'clock till 9½.   No Ladies admitted without Cards of Invitation.
> WESTFIELD, APRIL 1, 1864.

Courtesy Westfield Athenaeum Westfield, Ma.

The announcement for the 1874 Whip Makers Ball is notable for two reasons. First, it illustrates the fact that the industry has undergone a generational change in its leaders. Absent are Hiram Hull, Hiram Harrison, James Noble Sr. and Jasper Rand, all of whom have since passed away. Likewise, Samuel Dow is missing due to his having departed the whip industry to become a florist and horticulturalist.

Courtesy Westfield Athenaeum, Westfield, Ma.

The second note of interest is the apparent growing involvement from firms external to Westfield. In addition to the expected listing of many of Westfield's established whip men, the honorary committee shows several prominent whip makers from outside Westfield including; H.A. Strong (Rochester, N.Y.), A.W. Coburn (Windsor, N.Y.), and R.M. Milliken (Baltimore, Md.). The ball, held in the Music Hall could be attended for $2.00 for a gentlemen and lady or 50 cents to attend from the Gallery only.

Parades

In addition to the Whip Makers Ball and associated events, the Whip companies also participated in the various parades held in the Westfield area.

Springfield, Mass. - 250th Anniversary Parade, 1886

Courtesy Westfield Athenaeum, Westfield Ma.

The reverse side of this photo by A.V. Brown of Springfield is inscribed 'Whip Celebration 1886' with a list of the men from the J.C. Schmidt Whip Co. More likely, it appears to be the J.C. Schmidt Whip Co. float in the parade celebrating Springfield's 250th year. The parade was May 26,1886 and the official parade bulletin listed the trade wagons representing businesses in the greater Springfield area as marching in the 7th through 10th divisions, with J.C. Schmidt Whip Company in the 10th division. J.C. Schmidt was the sole participant representing Westfield, an acknowledgement of the importance of Whip manufacturing as Westfield leading industry.

Westfield, July 4, 1881-89 ?

Another photo exhibiting a whip company preparing for a parade is that of Sanford Whip. This undated this photo appears to be from the 1880's. The flags adorning the wagon have thirty-eight stars which were used from 1877 until July 4, 1890 when the forty-three star flag was adopted. Sanford Whip was founded and 1880 and the flags would indicate it was prior to 1890.

Courtesy Westfield Athenaeum, Westfield, Ma.

Westfield Park Square 1890's – Fourth of July

The following picture from the 1890's appears to have been taken circa 1893-1900 for a Fourth of July parade.

This photo was resurrected from an old negative in the Westfield Athenaeum archives showing Broad Street looking south with the Park Square Green on the right.

The exact location can be verified by the sign for the Nash Bakery on the left which was located at 8-9 Broad Street. Additionally, the date must be later than mid-1893 due to U.S. Whip's float in the lower right corner with U.S. Whip having been established on Dec. 29, 1892.

The identification of it most likely being a fourth of July parade is due to the man on the U.S. Whip float being dressed as Uncle Sam as would be typical for July 4th.

Courtesy Westfield Athenaeum, Westfield, Ma

Life as a 'Drummer'

The salesmen sent out by the whip companies were often called 'drummers', presumably for their role of drumming up business for the shops. Several of the larger companies had sales offices in New York and Boston but s significant amount of their orders came from these traveling salesmen. In addition to gathering orders for whips, the salesmen would have a supply of whips with them for immediate sales.

The sales trips for the drummers/salesmen could involve weeks or even months of time spent on the road. Leonard Atwater, a Russell native, started his career as a whip salesman, later becoming a prominent whip manufacturer in Westfield. Leonard Atwater's obituary in 1908 included the following notation:

> "He was one of the early whip salesmen who went out with large teams for trips of long duration and in 1840 Mr. Atwater went as far west as Ohio with a load of his goods."

As the industry grew, the whip companies would expand their sales efforts further and further west resulting in even longer trips. A *Springfield Republican* newspaper article of Jun. 11, 1885 made note of one of these trips.

> "One of the members of the Sanford whip company recently made what is probably the longest trip ever gone over by any Westfield 'drummer.' It was 15,000 miles long, extending from Canada to Texas and on the Pacific Coast from Mexico to British Columbia, including in it nearly every large city or town in almost all the states and territories west of the Hudson River, being nearly a four-month journey."

The *Three Oaks Press* of Three Oaks Michigan summarized a trip on June 24, 1892 by two of the Warren Featherbone Company employees as follows:

> "J.H. Ames of the Featherbone Company and C.H. Clark of the whip company arrived home on Tuesday evening from their long trip to California and the Pacific Coast sites. They have been gone over two months and" --- (illegible)--- " on Featherbone dress stays and whips in seventeen different states and territories and one foreign country as they crossed over from Texas into the Republic of Mexico. The exact distance traveled in making the trip was 7,000 miles."

In the above trip, the Warren Featherbone Company paired salesmen representing the two distinctly different operations of the company, both of which used 'featherbone' as a whalebone replacement. J.H. Ames represented the women's corset manufacturing portion of the business, while C.H. Clark was part of the whip operations. The reference to C.H. Clark was Charles H. Clark who would later relocate to Westfield and re-establish the Featherbone whip name in 1910.

While the development of railroads in the mid-1800's improved transportation and the ability to ship goods such as whips across the country, the use of traveling salesmen directly selling or taking orders from town to town was still a common method of doing business into the 20th century.

This undated postcard depicts a whip salesman getting ready to embark on a trip. Similar to other traveling salesmen of the time, the drummer would often sell other goods on his travels. While undated, the photograph is likely from the late 1890's to early 1900's, even though it is 'divided back' postcard indicating it was issued after 1906.

Published by J. E. W. Smith, Rochester, N. H.   Cart and Driver
Courtesy Westfield Athenaeum, Westfield, Ma

Another example of a traveling whip salesman is the following undated photo from the Westfield Athenaeum archives showing Edwin A. Warner, a 50 year whip salesman from Westfield.

Courtesy Westfield Athenaeum, Westfield, Ma

The photo is estimated as being circa 1870 based on: 1) The clothing in the picture being appropriate for the Civil War era or shortly thereafter, 2) Edwin A. Warner, born in 1832, would have been 38 years old in 1870. His appearance in the picture would also be appropriate for that time.

Edwin Alonson Warner, born in Granville Mass, lived in Westfield on Orange St. from the early 1870's until his death on May 4, 1909. City directories listed him simply as a Whip Agent and in later years, a Whip Dealer. His occupation on his death certificate was Whip Salesman. However, none of the documents listed which whip concerns he was employed at as a salesman. Based on the fact he was in the trade for 50 years, he likely was engaged by several firms over the course of his career. He is buried with his family in Pine Hill Cemetery, Westfield.

The life of a whip salesman was undoubtedly long and hard. The high turnover rate and difficulty in retaining good whip salesmen was highlighted in a United States Whip Company annual report on Dec. 18, 1901 by George Whipple, U.S. Whip President. In that report, Whipple stated there were 86 salesmen at the beginning of 1899. However, in the following year, 42 dropped out. Two years later the sales force was 115 men, a net increase of 31 salesmen. However, during that interval, the company had to hire and try out 174 men to compensate for the high turnover rate due to men quitting or new hires simply not succeeding.

Women owners of Whip related firms

While ownership of the whip shops was almost exclusively dominated by males, there were two women who are known to have operated their own businesses in the 1880's. Etta C. Ames and Lucinda (Stevens) Fuller were both listed in city directories as manufacturers of whip snaps.

Etta Ames was the first to be listed in the city directories beginning in 1886 with her whip snap shop located at 27 West School Street, where she remained throughout her listings. Her final listing as a snap manufacturer in the city directories was in 1893.

The second woman, following Etta C. Ames by one year, was Lucinda (Stevens) Fuller who was listed simply as Mrs. A. D. Fuller in the city directory business listings under whip snap makers. At her first listing of 1887, she was located at the rear of 198 Elm Street staying there until 1893. Lucinda relocated to 27 & 29 Chapel Street for one year in 1894, before moving to 32 Chapel Street, remaining there until her final listing in 1898. Lucinda Stevens Fuller passed away on Aug 28, 1898 at the age of 67 years, 8 months.

The 'Combination'

One of the earliest accounts regarding an effort to organize the whip makers of Westfield appeared in a *Springfield Republican* article on Nov. 23, 1865 reporting that the journeymen whip makers of Westfield had formed an organization for their mutual benefit, protection and intellectual improvement.

However, none of the elected officers were the owners of the major whip companies. It appears that the smaller firms were already experiencing the effects of being over taken by the more powerful companies and this was an attempt to protect themselves. No further mention of this group has been found and it appears to have dissolved shortly after.

By the early 1870's, the larger whip companies were becoming more organized as an industry. On July 12, 1874 the so-called 'Manufacturer's Co-Operative Association' elected the following officers: President, Ephraim Crary; Secretary & Treasurer, R.B. Robinson; Directors, E. Crary, L.B. Blood, E.B. Gillett, M.B. Whitney, Dexter Avery, E.R. Van Deusen and William Provin. What distinguished this group from the 1865 journeymen is the fact it was an organization now being run by many of the more significant whip manufacturers versus the tradesmen.

This organization was commonly referred to as the 'Combination'. The association was formed as a vehicle for the manufacturers to gather annually and establish rules and a pricing schedule for all of its members to abide by. By today's standards, many of the actions and intentions of this organization regarding price fixing and other practices would be a violation of anti-trust rules. However, in its day, it was similar to actions taken by many industries of that era.

At the same time the Combination was getting organized, American Whip Co. would start a series of acquisitions further establishing itself as the dominate whip company.

The first change would be in 1868 when Henry J. Bush, Rueben E. Noble, William O. Fletcher and Liverus Hull bought out the remaining investors. Soon after that, the company merged with the Van Deusen brothers, continuing under the name of American Whip. Subsequent acquisitions included; Rand, Lewis & Rand (1870), H.J. Bush Whip Co. (1870), and Westfield Whip Co. (1873).

By the time the Combination was established, Westfield's manufacturing base was already larger than the combined total of all the firms outside of Westfield. With the majority of the association's officers being Westfield men, the annual meetings being held in Westfield and the dominance in terms of manufacturing base, Westfield's position as the base for the entire whip industry was cemented.

The Combination was not without its trials and tribulations. The era of the mid-late 1800's was still a very volatile time caused by several factors including rising costs for materials, severe competition both within its membership and from external firms, and the ongoing pressures caused by a fluctuating economy.

The alliance of the whip companies at times resembled a marriage of convenience when they needed to cooperate during difficult times only to have one or more members take liberties compromising the agreements when individual business pressures arose. The association was abandoned several times, only to be reformed a year or two later.

By the mid 1870's the list of companies participating in the annual meetings included virtually every major whip manufacturer in the United States. The major firms external to Westfield who were regular participants in the annual meetings included:

J. H. Milliken	Baltimore, Md.
Woodbury & Co.	Rochester, N.Y.
Coburn Whip	Windsor, N.Y.
C.M. Comstock	Windsor, N.Y.
Wells Whip	Wellsville, Pa.
Weaver, Bardall & Humphrey	Moundsville, W.Va.
Dayton Whip	Dayton, Oh.
Tipp Whip	Tippacanoe Oh.
Underwood Whip	Sydney, Oh.
Featherbone Whip	Three Oaks, Mi
Michigan Whip	Hastings, Mi.
Binghampton Whip	Binghampton, N.Y
Buffalo Glove Co.	Windsor, N.Y.

Virtually all of these companies or their successors would become part of the consolidation of whip manufacturers in Westfield beginning in the early 1890's.

In 1876, the Combination appeared to have fallen apart again when newspaper accounts reported the whip makers council had adjourned with no association formed. However, it was also reported that all agreed to abide by a price schedule to be established by an appointed committee to be furnished to manufacturers, jobbers and retailers throughout the country.

The members of the appointed committee once again reaffirmed the connection between Westfield and the whip firms located elsewhere. The committee included: Robert F. Parker (Cook & Parker Whip), Charles C. Pratt (Hampden Whip) and Hial Holcomb (Holcomb & Cook) of Westfield. While,

H. N. Strong (Strong & Woodbury, Rochester) and P.H. Owen (Owen Bros., Windsor N.Y.) spoke for the outside firms.

The Combination would continue its tumultuous existence throughout the late 1870-80's. Various newspapers reported in 1881 about talks of potential dissolution of the Combination due to non-members selling their goods at prices far below the established schedule the members were expected to abide.

In Oct. 1882, newspaper accounts regarding an attempt to reestablish the association confirmed it had once again fallen apart. The talks about reforming the group continued through 1883.

Finally, on Oct. 7, 1886, an announcement of establishing the National Whip Making Association was made with E. R. Lay, President (Lay Whip, Westfield); Vice Presidents; S. Baker (Wells Whip Co., Wellsville, W. Va.), E.K. Warren (E.K. Warren Featherbone Whip, Mich.), Secretary, Merritt Van Deusen (Van Deusen Bros., Westfield); and Treasurer, R. F. Parker (Cook & Parker, Westfield).

A theme consistent with other announcements for the whip association, was that the object of the organization was to prevent a continuance of the profitless competition which had resulted from the lack of an organization and associated price list. The association was meant to include not only the manufacturers but also the dealers of supplies for their raw goods such as whalebone, rattan, leather, thread, etc.

Less than a year later in July 1887, the Combination fell apart yet again after allegations that agents for the association's president were violating the price schedule agreements. The newspaper articles did not identify the man by name but from the Oct. 1886 announcement, this would have been Edwin R. Lay. Contributing to the problem was a significant error made by the association regarding when the schedule would take effect. The agreement allowed for manufacturers to continue selling their goods at any price they chose until the establishment of the association was finalized. The problems caused by some of the members not abiding by the agreement resulted in the association rescinding the price schedule which effectively dissolved the Combination due to its having been the very foundation on which it was established.

Newspaper articles in early August, claimed to have uncovered the reasons the Edwin R. Lay Co. felt they were free to negotiate their own prices. According to the reports, Edwin Lay claimed American Whip, Sanford Whip and Woodbury & Strong had committed to pay them $12,000 to offset losses they might incur by joining the association. Supposedly, American Whip refused to agree, at which point Edwin Lay felt they were out of the pool and free to negotiate for themselves. By the time an agreement for a $5,000 per month payment to E.R. Lay was reached, the company had been operating outside of the association rules for several months. thus, leading to the discord which ended up with the breakdown of the association.

The role of American Whip in the affairs of the Combination aren't clear. On the contrary, throughout the duration of the Combination there was virtually no mention of American Whip. Its officers were also never mentioned as leaders in the efforts. In fact, it's very possible American Whip was already so dominate that it may not have been in their best interests in having their competition organize and become more competitive.

Surviving in a tough economic era

The economy of the country during the mid-late 19th century had a significant effect on the whip industry and undoubtedly contributed to the difficulty in maintaining the national organization. As the economy waxed and waned, there would be periods of high prosperity soon to be followed by times of little to no activity. Reports of factories running on full-time or greater, were often soon followed by periods where reports of half time or even plants shutting down would occur. The erratic nature of the business cycles undoubtedly contributed to the high turnover rate and demise of many of the smaller firms.

During times of high activity, the larger companies would build their inventories. Then, during low or stagnant business activity, the large firms having stockpiled their inventories could simply shut down manufacturing, having the capital and inventory to ride out the lean times until business improved. The larger firms were also often run by the same men that were the officers and directors of Westfield's banks having significant investments in Westfield's other industries such as cigars to buffer them. The smaller companies were not so fortunate and suffered more immediate consequences often resulting in closures, the need to merge with other partners to survive or sometimes being consumed by the larger companies.

The pressures on the companies to continue selling their goods even during lean times undoubtedly was a factor leading to firms not abiding by the rules of the Combination. The companies began cutting prices and doing whatever they needed to do to remain in business. This naturally led to a conflict between the less affluent firms and those who were on a stronger financial footing.

One example of how stagnant economical periods strained companies was the demise of Hampden Whip Company in 1883. In the later part of 1883, the economy and whip trade were both experiencing another of period of difficult times. Most of the whip companies in Westfield had shut done completely in the fall of that year. In December, newspaper accounts reported that one or two companies had reopened the previous week but were still not on full-time. The reports also stated it was unlikely that American Whip would resume operations for another month.

However, American Whip in spite of the slow economic times purchased Hampden Whip, its customer base, machinery and $40,000-50,000 worth of finished goods already on hand. The acquisition of Hampden Whip's inventory added to American's stockpile of finished goods without incurring the expense of resuming operations. In short, American Whip had the resources to effectively exploit the poor economy, capitalize on one of their largest competitor's financial difficulties and strengthen their own company, further enhancing their position of power in the industry.

By the mid 1880's, within Westfield there was a growing division amongst the whip companies with the evolution to a very few large whip companies and a much larger number of significantly smaller firms. The disparity in the size of the whip companies can be seen from data taken from the *Statistics of Manufacturers in Massachusetts – 1888.* While the statistics were a Massachusetts wide accounting, considering that aside from a few very small shops being located outside of Westfield by this time, the data is almost exclusively attributable to Westfield. Additionally, the total number of firms accounted for (60) is very close to the number of companies listed as Whip related firms in the 1888 Westfield City directory.

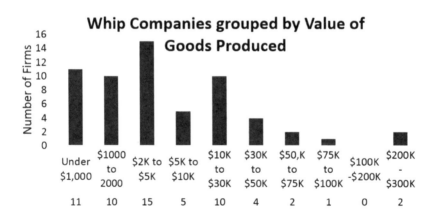

Based on the value of whips produced, the five largest companies produced over 60% of the total value of whip related goods produced in Westfield. The report didn't specify the firms by name but based on data from other sources, the largest would have been American Whip, with the next four most probably William Provin, J.C. Schmidt, Edwin Lay Whip Co. and Steimer, Searle & Co.,

Conversely, 60% of the firms (36) produced an average value of $5,000 or less yearly.

Employment starts shifting to other Industries.

The 1890 *Gazetteer of Massachusetts* documented various statistics for the towns and cities of Massachusetts based on data gathered by the state in 1885. Westfield's employment statistics for manufacturing were as follows:

	Employees	% of Mfg. Employees
Whips	481	33
Cigar and tobacco	386	26
Manufacture of Iron Goods	257	18
Paper Making	171	12
Manufacture of Cigar Boxes	36	2.5
Coffin Trimmings	46	3.2
Making Piano Legs	36	2.5
Making Organs	26	1.8
Totals	1449	

Despite the whip industry being at its peak, the 1885 statistics illustrate how whip employment was beginning to decline both in raw numbers and the percentage of persons employed compared to Westfield's overall workforce engaged in manufacturing.

One of the key contributors to the decline was likely the improvements with the machinery used in the manufacture of whips. While the production volumes continued to rise, the modernized factories needed less people to run them.

The reported statistics also give some insight to the industries which were growing and providing employment to the workers who may have been displaced by the changing whip industry. The introduction of new businesses to employ the shrinking whip workforce would become a critical issue as the industry declined after 1900.

Another important statistic from the table is the number of employees attributed to the manufacture of iron goods. While the number of employees working on whips and cigar was important at almost 60% of the workforce, it is combination of many companies. The 257 employees accounting for almost 20% of the workforce was a single company, being the H. B. Smith company. H. B. Smith would outlive both the whip and tobacco industries becoming one of Westfield's major businesses for over 100 years.

The Whip 'Syndicate' - beginning of the consolidation

Rumors about a possible whip syndicate began circulating in 1890 when an article of March 23, 1890 in the *Springfield Republican* described a proposal for creation of what was called the "Whip Syndicate". How much of the article is accurate and how much was merely a grandiose prediction is questionable.

However, it heralded the beginning of reports which would not be culminated until almost 3 years later with the establishment of the United States Whip Corporation.

The headline of the Article read:

> *"FORMATION OF A WHIP SYNDICATE*
> *A Big Scheme Thus effects Westfield People – Purpose and Prospects of the Project – A Scare over costly paying"*

Reportedly, Ralph D. Gillett, a well-known Westfield businessman, came up with the idea for the whip syndicate. His plan was to form an organization similar to what other industries of that era were using during that time via syndicates or consolidation. Early in the article it was stated that all of the major whip concerns, both in Westfield and elsewhere, had already signed an agreement to join the syndicate. However, examining the article in detail, it's apparent several liberties were being taken with the true facts. R.D. Gillett had supposedly visited all of the largest whip factories outside Westfield 'within a week'. This would have been virtually impossible given that it would have required significant meetings at each location and the locations were spread out across several states including Massachusetts, New York (4), W. Virginia, Ohio, Maryland, Michigan and a few others.

Much later, the article stated that the Westfield agreement was contingent upon the external companies all agreeing to the plan, contradicting the initial statement that all of the firms both within Westfield and external to Westfield were already onboard.

The article also claimed that 'So much confidence is felt in the scheme by the manufacturers that the greater share of the capital stock has been snapped up by them.' This would have been an interesting occurrence since it was still a conceptual idea with no actual company having been formed. Thus, there couldn't have been any stock to acquire.

In spite of the inconsistencies with the facts, the article does touch on several key reasons why consolidation made sense and what the driving factors were.

Namely:
- The whip manufacturers had been experiencing decreased profits for many years because of increasing manufacturing costs and price increases for their raw good such as whalebone, rattan, hides, etc. As such, the article stated the intent wasn't to advance whip prices, rather the goal was to improve profits by reducing the costs to manufacture the whips.

- The members of the syndicate (both suppliers and manufacturers) would be able to: reduce the risk of bad debts, be guaranteed a secure known price for their goods and rely upon their accounts being paid promptly by supplying their goods directly to the syndicate.

- The syndicate would also control the flow of raw goods by having their suppliers give bonds to only furnish goods to persons inside the syndicate or they would be boycotted.

- The text also documents that the multiple competing firms were all maintaining their own staff of salesman, also called drummers. Eliminating these redundant workforces would significantly reduce sales costs.

However, the final lines of the article hint that there were possibly clouds on the horizon with its concluding statement.

> "The scheme is a big affair and not a few of those who have been quietly kept posted as to its progress are skeptical as to its success, but on the other hand shrewd businessmen support the plan and say it can be made to operate and prove a good thing to all concerned."

The skepticism alluded to in the article proved itself to be true on April 10, 1890, when newspapers reported that the proposed merger which had been widely publicized a mere 3 weeks earlier, was being completely abandoned by R.D. Gillett, "when the failure of one or two firms to comply with all the requirements set things running on a contrary course." The firms causing the agreement to fall apart were not named. B it is likely that American Whip being the largest whip firm and least likely to benefit from relinquishing any of its control over the industry was one of the firms behind the failure of the proposal.

Less than 2 months later, another rumor began circulating stating an English syndicate was attempting to buy the entire whip industry. On May 8, 1890 the *Springfield Republican* published the rumor in a simple article as follows:

> "An English syndicate is now said to be trying to buy-up and control the whip business of the country and have its headquarters at Westfield."

Articles with a similar message appeared in Rochester, N.Y., Three Oaks Michigan and several other cities where other whip companies were located. Some of the articles went a step further stating that some firms had already been purchased by the English syndicate which proved to be in error.

On May 11, 1890, the Springfield papers published a longer and more in-depth article describing a supposed visit in Westfield by a New York agent representing the English group. The proposal was a plan to consolidate the United States whip firms into an organization with a capital value of $1,000,000. Reportedly, 60 % of the stock would be controlled by the English with 40% remaining in the United States. The whip men were to submit their business information to an expert and also respond with a price which they would be willing to accept to dispose of their business. The article further stated the Westfield manufacturers were thinking it over and further developments may be expected soon.

The very next day, May 12, 1890, the *Boston Herald* reposted a summary of the Springfield article and made what must have been one of its largest typographical errors of its time, when it incorrectly reported the value of the proposal as being $100,000,000.

The English syndicate rumor/proposal while published widely and for a longer period than the Gillett proposal, also fell by the wayside. No further rumors regarding consolidation and buyouts were widely reported until the spring of 1892.

Consolidation plans resurfaced in April of 1892 when the *Springfield Republican* published an article on the 28th, with the headline:

> "TO UNITE ALL WHIP FACTORIES
>
> Westfield Makers asked to Join in a corporation
> to control the product in the United States"

The article began with stating an attempt was being made to consolidate all of the whip concerns under a single management. A gentleman by the name of C.C. Foster of New York City was reportedly engaged in presenting the proposal. Mr. Foster said his plan was meeting with general favor and he believed he could secure the outcome desired.

The article goes on to highlight there were several areas of concern which had driven costs up and restated the fact there had previously been several failed attempts to consolidate the firms. Many of the relevant points for the need to consolidate were the same as those originally described in the article of March 20, 1890. The article also described C. C. Foster's rationale for why his proposal was feasible.

It was also acknowledged that some of the companies external to Westfield such as those in Rochester, N.Y. and Columbus, Ohio still needed to be consulted but it was believed that they could all be brought into the big corporation.

In yet another example of poor reporting of the facts, on the very next day, the *Worcester Spy* misrepresented the story saying New York parties had secured the consent of the 15 whip manufacturers of Westfield to sell their works to a syndicate. While the Worcester article did touch upon a couple points made in the more expansion Springfield report, it did not include any of the details provided by C. C. Fosters comments. Their proclamations that the agreement was secured was obviously premature as no further activity appeared to take place for several months. However, unlike previous attempts, C.C. Foster's proposal didn't fade away.

The deal appeared to have stalled by December 4, 1892, when newspaper accounts were reporting the proposed whip combination was not receiving any attention outside the whip firms. The articles further went on to state that with the lack of progress on the merger, the local whip manufacturers were caught in the middle, not knowing whether they would be swept up in the merger or whether to plan business as usual for the coming year. C.C. Foster was supposed to be coming to Westfield for further discussions. Foster was also reported as traveling for weeks all over the country trying to secure financial backing as he continued to drive his plan forward.

Meanwhile, the outside press and general public were kept in the dark regarding discussions regarding the whip syndicate. Yet another inaccurate newspaper article regarding the syndicate was published on Dec 25, 1892 when a *Springfield Republican* newspaper article reported in part......

> "To all appearances the whip syndicate has taken a decided funk. For months the matter has been under consideration, and Mr. Foster has been traveling about the country attempting to arrange the details of the scheme or getting sufficient backing to start the combination. So much time has been consumed that many of the whip men have become convinced that there is no hope for the

formation of the syndicate and freely express their concerns on the subject."

Four days later, on Dec. 29, 1892, while not as expansive as originally speculated, the deal was consummated with the incorporation of the United States Whip Corporation.

Modern Era (1893 – Present)

While acquisitions and mergers had a long history in the whip industry, the establishment of United States Whip Co. ushered in a new era of acquisitions. An ongoing consolidation of the industry would continue until 1921 when U.S. Whip made its final major acquisition of New England Whip.

Ironically, the establishment of United States Whip and the associated acquisitions and consolidation of the industry which followed soon after, coincided with the singular event which would intimately lead to its demise, namely the introduction of the automobile. The first automobile to be assembled in neighboring Springfield were the Duryea's which was also launched in 1893. It would be many years before the automobile industry significantly cut into the whip industries but by the early 1900's its growing impact was unmistakable.

United States Whip Corporation formed, Dec. 29, 1892

After years of discussion the great merger was finally consummated. However, several significant events occurred which changed the complexion of the new corporation from what had originally been publicized.

First, the whip men removed themselves from Westfield for the establishment of the new corporation. United States Whip was officially organized in Maine, in a meeting held at 39 Exchange St. in Portland on Dec 29, 1892. Why the whip manufacturers wanted to have the corporation based in Maine instead of Massachusetts isn't clear. It was possibly for tax reasons or as a legal vehicle to avoid assuming liabilities when acquiring the firms established in Massachusetts and other states.

Of the original seven men who signed the organization papers, five were Westfield Whip makers. Four of these men, James R. Noble Jr., Lewis Parker, Ira Miller and L.R. Norton were officers of American Whip. Edwin L. Sanford, president of Sanford Whip Co. rounded out the Westfield contingent. The other two incorporators were Charles C. Foster and Walter C. Cogswell both of Boston. Absent were any English or New York investors or men who ran whip companies external to Westfield. In reality, the nucleus of US Whip's management came directly from American Whip. C.C. Foster and Walter C. Cogswell were not whip makers. Charles C. Foster was an investor/businessman and Walter C. Cogswell a lawyer.

The corporation was formed with a capital stock value of $2,200,000 with 22,000 shares of stock @ $100/share in its registry. The seven men signing the papers were documented as owning one share each at $100.00/share. Thus, the largest whip firm in the world for a very brief period was started on a $700.00 outlay as a formality to finalizing the creation of the corporation.

With the establishment of the new company, United States Whip inherited the dominant role of the industry from American Whip and would retain that position for another 30 plus years. In the end, American Whip effectively used consolidation as leverage to acquiring several of its competitors.

On Jan 4, 1893, the *Springfield Republican* issued a list of companies expected to become a part of United States Whip which was widely republished by major newspapers across the country. However, as had been the case with previous reports, this list was not only premature but overly optimistic. The acquisitions would take several years with several large firms on the list remaining independent.

As new companies were brought in to the fold, the former presidents or managers of the larger firms typically became members of the board of directors. The monies they received also enabled them to become the major stockholders of the company as well.

Newspaper reports were projecting virtually every Whip company in Westfield and most major firms outside of Westfield were to be part of the new 'syndicate'. However, while extensive, the list of targeted companies was much more focused. The following chart was compiled from the U.S. Whip ledgers of Jan & Feb of 1893, listing the companies they were targeting for acquisitions and the values of each firm where documented.

It should be noted that the Westfield firms of New England Whip, Cargill, Cook & Co, Cook & Parker and Pomeroy & Van Deusen, all of whom were significant whip shops and competitors of U.S. Whip, were not listed in the U.S. Whip ledgers, implying they were not targets for takeover. Additionally, several of the companies, which had authorized acquisition values did not initially become branches of U.S. Whip.

Companies from Westfield

	Value in $	Acquired 1893-94
American Whip	500,000	X
Sanford Whip	125,625	X
Lay Whip	103,000	X
Massasoit	71,000	X
Standard Whip	55,000	
Baystate Whip	53,200	X

	Value in $	Acquired 1893-94
W.H. Owen	50,000	
L. H. Beals	49,500	
Peck & Whipple	44,000	X
J. C. Schmidt	31,900	X
Steimer & Moore	27,500	
Geo E. Whipple	22,000	X
Westfield Whip	21,250	X
Searle Whip	21,150	
Edmund Cooper	2,400	
A. Dibble	1,650	

Companies external to Westfield

	Value in $	Acquired 1893-94
Weaver, Bardall & Humphrey Mfg. Co., Moundsville, W. Va.	192,500	
Coburn Whip Co., Windsor, N. Y.	99,000	X
Tipp Whip Co., Tippecanoe Ohio	93,500	
Featherbone Whip Co., Three Oaks Michigan	74,264	
Buffalo Glove and Whip, Buffalo, N.Y.	71,500	
Michigan Whip Co., Hastings Michigan	60,500	
J. H. Milliken & Sons, Baltimore, Md	49,500	X
C M. Comstock Co., Windsor New York	49,500	X
Dayton Whip Company, Dayton, Oh.	29,691	
Keystone Whip & Net Co., Wellsville, Pa	23,056	
York Whip Co, York, Pa.	15,400	
John Dennes, York, Pa	8,500	

L H Luddick, York, Pa	6,600	
Woodbury & Co. , Rochester, N.Y.		
Wells Whip Co., Wellsville Pa.		X
Underwood Whip Co., Sydney Ohio		X

To manage the financials for the acquisitions, U. S. Whip appointed Walter G. Cogswell, a Boston lawyer (and one of the initial seven incorporators) as trustee to manage the acquisition funds. While production volumes, employee numbers and other details were not recorded, these figures can be used to understand the relative sizes of the various companies.

The list of potential acquisitions explains the basis for why U.S. Whip was incorporated with a capital stock value of 2.2 million dollars consisting of 22,000 shares at $100 per. The total value of the companies if they were all acquired at the assessed value is equal to $ 1,995,378. Wells Whips and Underwood Whip were not included in the companies for which Cogswell was to manage the funds, presumably those transactions had already been completed and their combined values would account for the remainder of the $2.2 million evaluation.

While the resulting consolidation didn't include all of the Westfield companies, it did take major strides towards achieving its goal of consolidating and controlling the industry. Prior to 1893, American Whip had already established itself as the dominant player in the industry. By the end of 1893, United States Whip was almost three times the original size of American Whip.

Immediately upon its formation, U.S. Whip announced that the 'branch' firms as the newly acquired companies were called, would continue to operate as independent firms. Most of the former owners/managers of the acquired companies also assumed positions as directors of the new corporation. For some twenty years after the formation of U.S. Whip, many of the 'branches' were still advertising and operating as if they were still manufacturing whips as their own companies.

Allowing the branches to continue operating as individual firms contradicted some of the fundamental reasons for consolidation. It negated the ability to eliminate redundant sales staffs, alleviate the increasing cost of materials by creating a single purchasing entity, and compromised the goal of eliminating unnecessary competition amongst the partners, all of which were the intended benefits to be achieved by consolidation.

An article of Dec 31, 1899 in the *Springfield Republican* noted; "The whip men of the town are holding conferences with the idea of bringing about some sort of agreement regarding the price of whips." The article further stated that competition has been fierce, prices were being cut to the extent that whips were almost being given away and efforts to establish price schedule both within the syndicate and outside had failed. Additionally, it was stated that conferences of this type had been held in the past with little success. Furthermore, the Spanish-American War was affecting the availability and cost of rattan, a critical resource for whip making.

In short, while the article doesn't explicitly state it, the establishment of U.S. Whip as a syndicate failed to achieve its desired result and there was little more control over the industry than prior to 1893.

The problems created with the inability to reduce sales forces due to the branches operating independently would come to the forefront nine years later when the 1901 annual report of George E Whipple, president of U.S Whip, highlighted the sales staff issue with a recommendation of reducing the number of branches as one means of addressing the problem of redundant sales and support staff.

Additional details on American Whip and United States Whip are included in the chapter on Whip Company profiles.

Survivors of the United States Whip formation

The established Westfield firms which survived the establishment of the United States Whip Corporation with its associated acquisitions in 1893 & 1894 included:

>Cargill & Cook Co.
>New England Whip
>L.H. Beals & Son
>Pomeroy & Van Deusen
>Steimer & Moore Whip
>Standard Whip / C.C. Pratt
>Cook & Parker
>A.C. Barnes
>Searle Whip Co.
>William Provin

The establishment of US Whip in 1893, began a period of acquisitions and consolidation as the of restructuring in the industry evolved.

As consolidations and acquisitions became more frequent, new companies continued to emerge, some of the more prominent activities included:

- 1894 saw the establishment of Independent Whip at 197 Elm St. The company moved to their new factory at 92 North Elm Street by 1903, where they would remain until being purchased by United States Whip.
- The Horse Whip company was the next new firm to be started. They were initially located on Thomas Street in 1901, moving to the rear of 287 Elm Street within a year.
- In 1903, John P. Pomeroy sold his interest in Pomeroy & Van Deusen Whip Co. to Henry M. Van Deusen. Van Deusen then changed the name of the firm to H.M. Van Deusen and Company.
- A.C. Barnes Whip Co. & Searle Whip merged in 1903, forming Woronoco Whip Co. only to dissolve one year later, with Barnes and Searle reestablishing their companies under their original names.
- Cargill, Cleveland and Co. was established in 1905 following the departure of A.J. Cook from Cargill, Cook & Co. A.J. Cook immediately established A.J. Cook & Co.
- New England Whip acquired Searle Whip in 1904 and Woodbury Whip of Rochester, N.Y. in 1907. The company then bought both L.H. Beals Whip Co. and Washington Whip Co. of Nashville, Tn in 1915
- Following the transactions by Independent Whip Co. and New England Whip Co., the United States Whip Co. made a series of acquisitions which completed the consolidation of the major firms including:

    1. 1918, Purchase of Independent Whip and its branches (International Whip, Continental Whip, Cowles-Horan & National Whip).

    2. 1919, Acquisition of Tipp Whip of Tippecanoe Ohio

    3. 1921, United States Whip makes its final major acquisition with the purchase of New England Whip and its branches. (Searle Whip, Woodbury Whip, L.H. Beals and Washington Whip)

With the final acquisition of New England Whip, United States Whip had acquired well over 30 Whip companies between 1893 and 1921, in addition to many smaller shops who specialized in specific goods. Many of the companies continued to be listed as branches into the 1920's, with whips sold under their labels, even though the bulk of the manufacturing was done in the main factory at 24 Main St.

The 1923 Westfield City Directory listed a total of thirty-five companies as whip manufacturers. In reality, the actual number of whip firms was a mere nine companies. Twenty-six of the companies listed in the 1923 City Directory existed in name only and are listed as branches of U.S. Whip at 24 Main St. New England Whip although still listed as being at 171 Elm St, had also already been acquired by U.S. Whip.

Of the remaining nine, three were smaller specialty shops. Charles W, Hassler had a specialty leather shop, N. F. Tyler produced a small number of whips but was primarily an agent for selling whips and machinery, while American Holly Whip specialized in manufacturing whips with wooden handles made from imported English holly.

The remaining six firms in order of their size were:

    United States Whip Company, 24 Main St.
    Cargill, Cleveland & Company, 177 Elm St.
    H. M. Van Deusen Co., 42-46 Arnold St.
    The Horse Whip Company, 171 Elm St.
    Standard Whip, 287 Elm St.
    Barry Whip Co., 360 Elm St.

After 1923, the number of whip companies listed in the city directories would continue to decline as more and more branches of United States Whip were retired or no longer actively advertised.

Barry Whip, re-established in 1923 after Maurice Barry was successful in a law suit against U.S. Whip, was actually contracting with Cargill & Cleveland & Co. to manufacture his whips. By 1926, Barry Whip Co. was listed as a branch of Cargill, Cleveland & Co.

The 1930 city directory listed only six companies as Whip Manufacturers;

    American Whip (branch of US Whip)
    Barry Whip (branch of Cargill, Cleveland)
    Cargill Cleveland & Co.
    Horse Whip Co.
    Tyler Whip Co.
    United States Whip Co.

Horace Avery, Whip Lash manufacturer, was the sole listing for any other Whip related business.

The Whip's final chapter as a major Westfield Industry.

As the whip industry gradually declined, one by one all of the original whip companies would succumb.

United States Whip ceased production of whips by the 1930's. U.S. Whip established a branch division of United States Golf in 1927 to manufacture golf equipment but it failed to survive after a few years. The United States Line Co. became their primary business, manufacturing fishing lines and becoming a distributor of associated fishing equipment. U.S. Line was sold in 1961 to Chester Cook Sr., Bradlee Gage and a small group of private investors with Chester Cook becoming the President and Bradlee Gage, Vice-President of the company at that time.

H. M. Van Deusen Co. located on Elm Street in the Allen Power Building next to the Green River Bridge moved to 42 Arnold Street by 1917 and operated there until 1930. Shortly after Henry Van Deusen's death on Mar 30, 1930, the company ceased operations and was liquidated in October of the same year. The Van Deusen building on Arnold Street later became the headquarters for Stanley Home Products and more recently was converted into one and two bedroom apartments.

The Horse Whip Company, initially located at 287 Elm Street in the Atwater building, relocated to the rear of 273 Elm Street by 1909. It next moved to 360 Elm Street in 1921 and finally to 171 Elm Street in 1923, where it remained until 1936 before it was formally dissolved in 1937.

Standard Whip, was initially located at 173 Elm St. at the rear of the Textile Mfg. Company Building. (aka Power Building). Standard Whip moved to 287 Elm in 1911. In 1924 the company name was changed to Advanced Whip and Novelty company and specialized in making small whips and novelty items for fairs. The company was forced to relocate to 350 Elm Street in 1924 after a fire ravaged their building at 287 Elm. Once the name was changed from Standard Whip to Advanced Whip & Novelty, the company stopped being listed as a whip manufacturer in the city directories.

Cargill, Cleveland and Company produced whips under their own name until 1952. Beginning in 1923 they also produced whips for the Barry Whip Company prior to it becoming a branch of Cargill, Cleveland & Co. In 1923, Cargill, Cleveland and Co. relocated from the Power building at 171 Elm Street to 360 Elm Street.

The final listing for Cargill, Cleveland at 360 Elm Street in the Westfield city directories was in 1952, by which time it had been purchased by Harold J. Martin who had established the Westfield Whip Manufacturing Co. in 1946.

The demise of these firms effectively ended Westfield's dominant position in the country's whip industry. More specifically for Westfield, it ended the local industry's role a as major employer or economic influence in the city.

The Westfield Whip Manufacturing Co. was left to carry the banner forward as Westfield's only significant maker of Whips.

Westfield Whip Manufacturing Company, Westfield's final Whip Company

Westfield's final whip company, Westfield Whip Manufacturing Company, was established in 1946 by Harold J. Martin. Westfield Whip Mfg. was initially located at 44 Court Street. By 1952 the company moved to 360 Elm Street in the former Cargill & Cleveland Co building with Harold Martin purchasing the company at that time. Westfield Whip Mfg. would operate continuously until 2018 when it began operating on a part time basis with a reduction in production.

In addition to the assets of Cargill, Cleveland & Co., Harold Martin purchased many of the old machines and records of the older now defunct companies both within and external to Westfield which have been stored in the current factory.

The only other whip company in Westfield during this time would be Edward Grudowski's small shop of Great American Leather Products. Great American was located at the rear of 34 Meadow Street from 1962 until 1966 before relocating to the Crescent Mills section of Russell.

For more details on the various whip companies refer to the individual profiles in the Chapter on Whip Company profiles.

The Longest Running Whip Companies in Westfield.

The continuum of American Whip and United States Whip from 1855 until approximately 1935 was Westfield's longest running whip manufacturer at 80 years.

Westfield Whip Manufacturing Co. established in 1946 by Harold J. Martin and carried on by his family, while not one of the largest firms, holds the distinction of being the longest continually running Whip factory under a single ownership operating for seventy-two years as of 2018.

The distinction of longest running whip operation from Westfield's earlier era doesn't belong to one of the larger companies. That honor resides with the Avery family, who for three generations operated their Whip lash company for sixty-six years. Horace W. Avery established his company at 170 Main Street as a maker of whip lashes by 1873. The company would remain in his name until he passed away in 1909 at the age of 78. His son, Frank H. continued the business at the same location for fifteen years before passing away July 29, 1923. At that time, a third generation of the Avery family, Horace W, grandson of the original Horace assumed operating the business. Horace would operate the whip lash business at that same location for another sixteen years before he too passed away on Aug 3, 1939.

Westfield's Whip District

While Westfield's whip industry during its heyday was the largest producer of whips in the world, the actual amount of geographical space it occupied in the central part of the town was actually quite small.

In the early years, there were pockets of whip makers and whip lash shops in the outlying sections of Westfield including; Mundale, Wyben/West Farms and Little River. Westfield's northeast section of East Mountain did not have any whip making of significance.

The Mundale area had the largest amount of early whip activity, followed by Wyben/West Farms, then Little River.

As the whip industry evolved into a modernized, factory-based industry, businesses were increasingly established in or relocated to the center of Westfield. By the late 1870's, the majority of the whip manufacturing factories were located within the area bounded by Main Street to the South, Mechanic Street on the East, Meadow Street to the North and on the West, roughly a block or two west of Elm Street including Franklin St. and Washington St.

The whip district shrank even more by 1900. United States Whip was at 24 Main Street. Independent Whip was the sole factory north of the river on North Elm Street. The remaining factories were mostly located on Elm Street between Franklin Street and the Westfield River, with a few smaller shops off Mechanic Street. By that time, virtually all of the factories were located on less than ¼ square mile of real estate.

The darker shaded area of the map denotes the area where the majority of major firms and factories were located. The lighter shaded area had numerous smaller shops, some operating in buildings that are currently residential homes.

Westfield's – Whip District

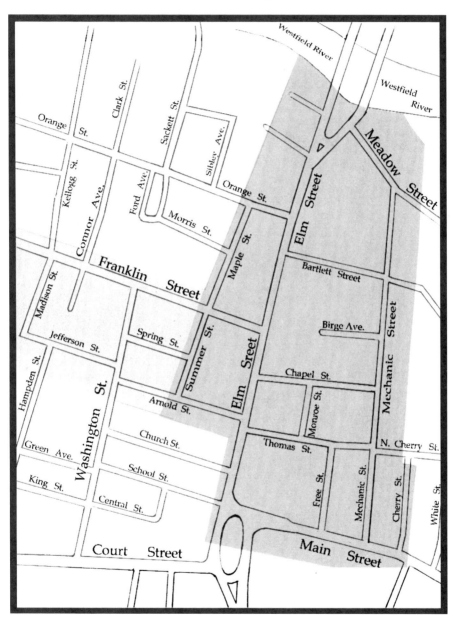

Westfield's Whip Industry in Pictures

While most of Westfield Whip factory buildings no longer exist, fortunately there are a few photographs, postcards and business/trade magazine illustrations to remind us of Westfield's whip heritage.

One of the most extensive series of pictures in a single compilation was published in *Western New England*, a monthly trade magazine published by the Springfield Massachusetts Board of Trade from 1910-1913.

The featured article in the February 1911 Edition was *The Whip City, Westfield's Annual Contribution Toward Moving the World, How Whips are Made* by Edwin W. Newdick. The article spanning several pages gave a background on Westfield's whip industry and included a series of pictures of United States Whip and other shops which are included here.

All photograph's from the 1911 *Western New England* issue were scanned courtesy of Ralph E. Cortis from his personal collection.

The lead picture for the article showed a view looking north on Elm Street with the trolley center and Park Square on the right.

THE BUSINESS STREET IN THE TOWN WHERE MOST OF THE WORLD'S WHIPS ARE MADE

THE PLANT OF THE BIGGEST WHIP MANUFACTURERS IN THE WORLD, THE UNITED STATES WHIP COMPANY

(The head offices and all the manufacturing plants are at Westfield, except the building shown at the extreme left of the picture, which is the company's branch at Sidney, Ohio)

115

Interior Views of United States Whip:

THE UNITED STATES WHIP FACTORY MAKES DAILY AN AVERAGE OF ABOUT TWENTY-FIVE THOUSAND WHIPS

THE MACHINES WHICH ROUND THE RAWHIDE

THE PLAITING ROOM IN THE UNITED STATES WHIP COMPANY'S FACTORY

A FEW OF THE FINISHED WHIPS IN THE STOCK ROOM OF THE UNITED STATES WHIP COMPANY

ANOTHER VIEW IN THE WESTFIELD FACTORY OF THE UNITED STATES WHIP COMPANY

IN THE RATTAN STORAGE HOUSE OF THE UNITED STATES WHIP COMPANY, THE WORLD'S LARGEST WHIP PRODUCERS

The following are artist depictions of New England Whip and Independent Whip from the same article.

THE FACTORY OF THE NEW ENGLAND WHIP COMPANY

The New England Whip building shown above (aka Textile Mfg. Co./Power Building) was located on Elm Street across from Franklin Street. The smaller building to the left was known as the Provin Block and as the home to William Provin Whip Co. from 1881 – 1902. While the Power Building has since been demolished, the Provin Building still exists on Elm Street next to the Railroad Trestle.

THE FINE PLANT OF THE INDEPENDENT WHIP COMPANY

Advertisements from *Western New England*, Feb 1911

Horse Whip Co.

New England Whip Company

The final two Ads for United States Whip were full page color ads. They were also the only two pages in the edition which were not black and white.

No. 25 R. MADRAS RAWHIDE—One-half length, black color, fine finish, two 12-ring combination buttons, rubber cap, linen lined and waterproof, Philadelphia snap

No. 50 R. BURMA RAWHIDE—Combination of rawhide and laminated steel, stocked from butt to tip, black color, fine finish, Japanned cap, three 6-stitch russet thread buttons, linen lined and waterproof, hand-made snap

No. 75 R. CEYLON RAWHIDE—Heavy stocked rawhide from snap through cap, black color, fine finish, Japanned cap, two 20-ring combination buttons, three feet rubber lining, English hand-made snap

No. 100 R. INDIA RAWHIDE—Heavy stocked rawhide from snap through cap, black color, fine finish, Japanned cap, two 8-stitch hand-made buttons, double cover and wire lined, linen loop, hand-made snap

THE ABOVE is an illustration of our ALL RAWHIDE LINE. We have no story to tell about the QUALITY, WEIGHT, STYLE and FINISH of our goods—they will prove all this on inspection, and we invite the closest examination, and do not fear the knife if you wish to cut the whips open. These GOODS are made on HONOR, and stand for what we say—the very best that can be made in their respective classes.

We will say, however, that OUR RAWHIDE CENTERS cannot be equalled by anybody. We tan our own Hides and make our own Centers, and use nothing but the very BEST COMMISSARIAT HIDES, bought from the English Army, cured in the best manner possible, imported direct by us, and use no Slaughters, Derbungas, or Deads, which are an inferior stock, in our Rawhide Centers. We are the only manufacturers that can warrant this. The ALL RAWHIDE LINE is all that the experience of over half a century can produce.

UNITED STATES WHIP CO.
WESTFIELD MASS.

OUR WHIP SPECIALTIES
Have a World-Wide Reputation

No. 331—6 ft. Black color, fine finish, assorted colors enameled loaded handles in package, japanned cap, two combination buttons, Philadelphia snap.

No. 500. Grant's Patent. 7-12 length, extra heavy stocked rawhide, black color, extra fine finish, seamless vulcanized rubber inner cover, rubber cushioned cap, two combination chased buttons, English hand silk snap, re-enforced loop, 4 1-3, 5, 5½, 6, 6½, 7 ft.

No. 471. "Manatee" extra heavy Sirenia center from snap through cap, black color, extra fine finish, japanned cap, two long buttons, rubber lined through, all silk hand made snap, re-enforced loop, 6, 6½, 7 ft.

No. 506. Heavy rawhide from snap through cap, black color, fine finish, three 6-stitch hand made buttons, vulcanized rubber inner cover, all silk English snap, re-enforced loop, 6, 6½, 7 ft.

No. 487. "The Pacific Slope." Extra heavy rawhide from snap through cap, black 6-plait giant double cover, rubber and wire lined, linen loop, japanned cap, two 6-stitch hand made buttons, re-enforced buckskin snap, 6, 6½, 7 ft.

No. 717—6½ ft. Extra quality rawhide from snap through cap, black color, fine finish, japanned cap, two thread buttons, 1 inch wound keeper, 6-plait genuine buckskin top, Philadelphia snap.

UNITED STATES WHIP COMPANY,
WESTFIELD, MASS.

End of *Western New England*, Feb 1911 Layout

Photographs and Postcards

American Whip Company

One of the earliest surviving pictures of the Whip factories is the picture of the American Whip Company identified as having been taken in 1865.

Courtesy Westfield Athenaeum, Westfield, Ma.

The photo could have been taken in 1866, at the very latest, based on the fact the construction of the Westfield Athenaeum in the fall of 1866 would have prevented a photograph being taken from the vantage point of this photograph.

The next photo shows both American Whip and the newly constructed Westfield Athenaeum circa 1867 - 1869. The estimate is based on the fact that the new library was completed in early 1867 and the American Whip factory suffered a major fire on May 7 of 1869. This can be verified as being the old factory by the existence of the cupola on top of the building which was gone in later pictures after the factory was rebuilt. As such the photo must have been taken after the fall of 1867 and before the fire of 1869.

Also, as can be seen, the close proximity of the two buildings shows how the earlier 1865 picture would not have been possible once the library was constructed.

American Whip & Westfield Athenaeum c. 1867-69

Courtesy Westfield Athenaeum, Westfield, Ma.

Alonzo Van Deusen Whip Factory c. 1865

The following photo of the "A. Van Deusen's Whip Factory" has been tentatively identified as the factory on Mechanic Street circa 1865.

When the Van Deusen factory on Mechanic St. was advertised for sale in 1870 the description of the factory was given as being 140 feet long, 30 wide, two stories and basement, on a never-failing stream of water of 8 or 10 horse power. While the description of the building is slightly smaller than previous reports it was still a substantial building and the description as appropriate for the picture.

Courtesy Westfield Athenaeum, Westfield, Ma.

Alonzo Van Deusen Whip Factory c. 1865

Most Photographed Whip factories

The most two most photographed whip factories in Westfield were those of Textile Company/Power Building on Elm Street opposite the Franklin Street intersection and the United States Whip Co. buildings on Main Street. While other factories found their way onto postcards, newspapers and trade magazines, no other factories were as widely published as these two buildings.

Textile Manufacturing Company / Power Company Building

The Textile Manufacturing Company/Power Building at 167-177 Elm Street, located across from Franklin Street was home to many different whip firms in its lifetime. A large 3 story brick building, it was the home for more whip companies than any other structure in Westfield.

The larger firms that operated out of this building at different times included, Searle Whip, New England Whip, Cargill, Cook & Co., Cargill, Cleveland &

Co., Peck & Whipple, and L.H. Beals & Co.. In addition to these large firms, many smaller whip and lash makers rented space and operated in this same building as their larger competitors.

The building was later known as the Robinson Reminder building and also the home of Kellogg Brush Co and M & M Sales.

Power Building - Opposite Franklin St. on Elm St. Circa 1899. Now Mobil Gas Station

Courtesy Westfield Athenaeum, Westfield, Ma.

While identified as circa 1899, a more accurate date for the photo is 1897. The telltale clue is the sign 'Geo. Mesick Lash Manufr.' on the right side of the building between the second and third floor windows.

Per the Westfield city directories, in 1896 the Mesick Bros. were located in the Provin Block building to the left of this building. For one year only, 1897, Mesick was located here at 167-177 Elm Street.

Westfield City Directory - 1897

Finally, by 1898, George A. Mesick was operating his lash factory on Crary Avenue. George A Mesick would leave the whip business in November of 1898 after selling his factory and purchasing the meat shop of Joseph A. Arthur on Elm Street.

The postcard below, c. 1905 -1910 is a common view of the Power Company building. Multiple versions of this card with different colorations and taken from different angles were published. The titles for the different cards included: Power Company Building, New England Whip, Woodbury Whip, and others depending upon which business was being promoted.

Author's Personal Collection

The age of this postcard can be estimated as being at least 1905 or later by virtue of the Cargill & Cleveland sign on the leftmost part of the building. Prior to 1905 the company was still Cargill, Cook & Co. after which A.J. Cook left to start a new business under his own name.

The section of the building where New England Whip Co. was located is an addition to the original structure as can be seen by the lighter shade of bricks. The New England Whip addition was built in late 1903 to accommodate the company's growth. As such, any images showing the building without the right-side portion would be mid-1903 at the latest.

On many cards, hand drawn business signs such as the following Woodbury whip card were added to promote that business. This card can be aged as 1910 or later, with Woodbury having relocated to Westfield in 1910. This image is not a 'real photo' of the Power Building and is an artist rendition created from a photograph, having had a significant amount of coloration and other cosmetic alterations.

Author's Personal Collection

United States Whip Co.

In addition to the previously illustrated pictures from the 1911 *Western New England* brochure, United States Whip company, by virtue of its being the dominant company in the Whip industry had its picture widely distributed in various publications and postcards The following postcards and picture are a few additional views of the US Whip complex.

Authors Personal Collection

Authors Personal Collection

RF-21 U.S.Whip Co. Main St.-Now from Third National Bank Parking lot on right to Sears on left
FROM THE ROSS CONNER COLLECTION

Courtesy Westfield Athenaeum, Westfield, Ma.

The above picture estimated as c. 1920 is from the Ross Connor collection showing the United States Whip building. The tall building on the left side of the picture is the former Second Congregational Church.

Independent Whip Postcard c. 1910

P4686   Independent Whip Co., Westfield, Mass.

Author's Personal Collection

Independent Whip, located at 92 North Elm Street would later become the home of Old Colony Envelope Co. The building in the rear is the Bryant Box Co. which would also later become part of Old Colony Envelope Co. The original Independent Whip building was expanded and the buildings were joined together.

H. M. Van Deusen Whip Co. - circa 1905

The H.M. Van Deusen Whip Co. was originally established as Pomeroy & Van Deusen, located in the S.A. Allen Power Building on the east side of Elm Street next to the Great River Bridge. The factory was damaged in the floods of 1927 & 1936. The flood of 1938 dealt the buildings it's final blow after which it was condemned and the remains were demolished.

The following picture is from the Westfield *Times and Newsletter, Special Trade Edition* of Oct. 6, 1897.

POMEROY & VAN DEUSEN'S WHIP FACTORY. *Photo by Coleman.*
Author's Personal Collection

The next image is another view of Van Deusen Whip & the S.A. Allen Building. This view is looking from the north side of the river towards downtown Westfield.

Also, while the postcard is labelled Van Deusen Whip factory, the sign on the building under the top row of windows is actually the Searle Whip company who were leasing space from the Van Deusen's and was co-located with the Van Deusen Whip company in the factory.

VAN DEUSEN WHIP FACTORY, ON GREAT RIVER, WESTFIELD, MASS.

Author's Personal Collection

42 Arnold Street, former home of Van Deusen Whip Co.

Author's Personal Collection

The Postcard of 42 Arnold Street shows the offices of Stanley Home Products in the 1940's. The front entry was an addition to the Van Deusen Factory. But the remainder of the building is unchanged from the way it was when the whip factory operated until 1930.

Bishop, Lay & Co. and C.W. Spencer Factories, c. 1873

Courtesy Westfield Athenaeum, Westfield, Ma

The above picture was taken circa 1873. The factory of C.W. Spencer on the right was located at 103 Elm Street. At that time, 103 Elm Street would have been at approximately the location of the current Hampden County District Court building. The factory of Bishop & Lay on the left, was one building removed from Franklin Street. The home of Ephraim Crary, on the corner of Elm & Franklin, was to the left of the Bishop & Lay building.

The photo can be dated via the following facts. Bishop Lay & Co only existed late 1871 until 1873. Additionally, a newspaper article on May 30, 1873 announced Ephraim Crary had rented his Elm St. factory formerly occupied by Darling Smith & Company to Bishop. Lay and Co. with their taking possession on that day.

The final event to possibly identifying the date of the photo was the death of Wilber Bishop of Bishop, Lay & Co. Wilber P. Bishop died of typhoid fever at the age of 26 years on Nov 20, 1873. With many of the employees appearing to be in formal attire and the women likewise, this photo was possibly taken at the time of his funeral. Following Bishop's death, Edwin Lay moved the company to the rear of 107 Elm St., operating as Edwin R. Lay & Co.

Darling, Smith & Co. - c. 1871

Darling, Smith & Co merged with the Westfield Whip Co. in Nov. 1872, which establishes the next photo as being prior to that. The location is thought to be on the east side of Elm Street just south of the railroad crossing. The shadows as shown on the building would not have been possible had the factories been located on the west side of Elm Street.

Courtesy Westfield Athenaeum, Westfield, Ma

The photo is tentatively identified as being June – July 1871 based on the circus advertisements in the lower right. The bottom right most advertisement is for Wooten & Haight's Circus and Menagerie. Wooten & Haight operated under that name for only one year, with their circus having toured the New England States in the month of June 1871, establishing an approximate date for the photo.

1874-1878 Hampden Whip

c. 1880. This photo of Hampden Whip from a Sterograph by M.O.T. Coleman of Westfield is circa 1874-1878. Hampden Whip was at 92-94 Elm Street during this time. (Notice the double front entrances to the building.) Also, the sun is from the left (i.e. South) placing the building on the West side of Elm St. By 1879 Hampden Whip was located at "Elm opp. Franklin" and the sun would have been from the opposite side if the photo was taken at a later date.

Hampden Whip Company c. 1874-78   Coleman

Courtesy Chris Erickson

1887 - Lay Whip Company

The following lithograph is from *Massachusetts Industries - 1887*. Although it is a lithograph versus a photograph, the image is very accurate. In 1903, the Lay Whip factory became the Church for Holy Trinity. After the current church was completed in 1910 the building became the home for their elementary school.

Lithograph from *Massachusetts Industries - 1887*

The image below is the old whip factory as it appears today on Elm Street. Holy Trinity Church is out of sight to the left.

Author's Personal Collection
Lay Whip Building - 2018

A. C. Barnes Whip Company c. 1901 -1904

The picture shows the A.C. Barnes with the building clearly as 360 Elm Street, the home of Westfield Whip Manufacturing Co. and the planned Whip museum.

However, the city directories never listed A.C. Barnes as being located at 360 Elm Street. The closest location where A.C. Barnes was listed was the Power Building on the corner of Elm and Meadow Streets from 1901-1904, which would have been across Elm Street from this building. Possibly A.C. Barnes was in both buildings and his mailing address for the company was the other building.

An interesting side note is that the new museum needing handicap access to the building is installing a ramp in the same location as the original walkway.

Courtesy Westfield Athenaeum, Westfield, Ma.

New England Whip – 1897

Most photographs of New England Whip are from after it had moved to Elm Street in the Power Company Building. This image from the *Westfield Times Newsletter, Special Trade Edition* on Oct 6, 1897 shows New England Whip's original location at what is now 22 Cherry Street.

NEW ENGLAND WHIP COMPANY'S PLANT.

Author's Personal Collection

National Mfg. Co., Whips and Lashes

The following photo is once again from the *Westfield Times Newsletter, Special Trade Edition* of Oct 6, 1897. National Manufacturing Co. was primarily a whip lash manufacturer founded by J.E. Mesick operated at 7 – 9 Birge Ave from 1894 until approx. 1900 before relocating to 22 Elm Street.

NATIONAL MFG. CO., WHIPS AND LASHES. *Photo by Coleman.*

Author's Personal Collection

Whip Company Profiles

This chapter on Whip company profiles has two distinct sections.

With American Whip and United States Whip being the backbone of the industry from 1855 until the 1930's further information has been provided focusing on those two firms in the first section.

The second section is a chronological listing of the larger and or longer running whip firms. Also included in this section are profiles of several of the more significant companies from other locations which were closely linked to Westfield and also became part of the consolidation of the companies in the 1890's and later.

A full listing of whip shops firms which summarizes the years of operation of both above the firms and many of the smaller shops is included in the Appendices.

American Whip Company, est. 1855

       Location: Main Street
       Employees: 1860 Fed. Census – 260 males, 200 females
                    1880 Fed Census – 65 males 25 females
                      Various reports 100-400

    As stated previously, the foundation of American Whip began in the 1820's with the establishments of the whip companies of Hiram Hull, Hiram Harrison, and Dow & Gillett.
    American Whip was established by the merger of those firms in early 1855 with Edward B. Gillett, electing to not become part of the new corporation and separating from Samuel Dow to establish his own company.

    The following legal notice announcing the first meeting of American Whip was posted for 3 days in the Springfield Republican from March 19-21:

"**Notice.** - The first Meeting of the subscribers to the stock of the American Whip Company (a Joint Stock Co. under the laws of 1851) will be holden at the Town Hall in Westfield on Monday, the 26th day of March Inst., at 2 o'clock in the afternoon, for the purpose of organization, choosing officers and transaction other business.
    Hiram Harrison
                                              Sam'l Dow
                                              Wm. O. Fletcher
Westfield, March 16, 1855   mar19 3d"

Hiram Harrison became the first president of the new company and served until 1865 when he resigned due to ill health. By this time his co-founders had already left the company. Samuel Dow had exited the whip business by 1861 to become Westfield's pre-eminent florist and horticulturalist. Hiram Hull had already passed away on Oct 2, 1861 at the age of 65, with his cause of death listed as paralysis.

After the departure of Hiram Harrison, Henry J. Bush was appointed to the presidency and would hold that title for three years.

The president and chief officers of American Whip would change multiple times over the next twenty-five years as ownership changes occurred, arrival of new key players, departures of others and changes brought on by acquisitions.

July of 1868 brought a change of ownership of the company when majority stockholders Henry F. Bush, W.O. Fletcher, Reuben Noble and Liverus Hull bought out the remaining investors for $250,000 which was reported to be equal to $135 per share of stock.

Shortly thereafter, the company merged with the Van Deusen Brothers Whip Co., bringing Alonzo and Mark Van Deusen onboard.

The disastrous fire of 1869 that destroyed their factory (see the chapter on fires), brought about more changes in leadership. During the time the factory was being rebuilt, Henry Bush and W.O. Fletcher sold their interests to the Van Deusen brothers. Following the departure of Bush and Fletcher, Alonzo Van Deusen assumed the presidency of American Whip.

American Whip became a public stock company in Jan of 1870 with a capital value of $250,000 with Alonzo Van Deusen remaining president and Reuben Noble treasurer.

Although Henry J. Bush was a majority stockholder in American Whip, he still operated the H.J. Bush Whip company. On Mar 25, 1870, the Springfield Republican reported that his firm had consolidated with American Whip, increasing the capital of American by $100,000.

The 1870's and 1880's would see American Whip make several acquisitions as it bought out competitors and further strengthened its position in the industry.

The acquisitions included:
* Rand, Lewis and Rand Co., which was originally established as Jasper Rand Co. in the 1830, was acquired in late January of 1870, marking the end of the Rand's involvement in the Whip industry.
* Westfield Whip Co. was the next acquisition in late November of 1873 Two of the principals of Westfield Whip, C.W. Darling, and W.O. Fletcher, would join American Whip. A third, James T. Smith would leave the group and form his own company (National Whip). Westfield Whip was reported to have employed 200 workmen with a company valuation of $80,000.
* December 1873 saw the acquisition of New Haven Whip Co. which employed about 20 hands. The fact that Henry J. Bush of American, had already been a large stockholder in New Haven Whip for several years undoubtedly influenced the acquisition.
* Hampden Whip became the next casualty in 1883 when American Whip took advantage of its strong financial footing and a poor economy to acquire its competitor.

The 1880 Federal Census reported that at any one time, the most hands employed was 100 for the previous year. This figure seems drastically low considering the number of acquisitions and Americans position in the industry whether this was an incorrect recording of the numbers or due to some other reason hasn't been established. That same census indicated the company ran at 100 percent production for 10 months and 2/3 time for 2 months, so a long economic downturn would not have accounted for the low numbers. The employment numbers of 1880 are indicative of multiple reports over many years where the number of employees varied widely depending upon the economic situation at any given point in time.

In late 1875, Alonzo and Mark Van Deusen, reportedly holding over 20% of American stock valued at $67,000, sold their interest in the firm, leaving American Whip and establishing a new company under the name of Van Deusen Bros. Whip Co. (see 1876 – Van Deusen Bros.)

Robert F. Parker succeeded Alonzo Van Deusen as president, Henry J. Bush became vice president and Reuben Noble, treasurer. Joining them as directors were: Charles W. Darling, Liverus Hull, W.O. Fletcher, Edward R. Gillett, E. Nelson, David C. Hull and Lewis R. Norton.

This management team would remain in control until 1883 when the Van Deusen brothers would once again re-enter the picture. The Van Deusen's had re-entered American Whip via the 1883 acquisition of Hampden Whip after the Van Deusen Bros. Co. merged with Hampden Whip in 1878.

It was about this time that Ira Miller, a native of Cadiz, Kentucky, who had twenty years of experience in the leather and saddle industry began purchasing stock in American Whip. Miller who had married Francis Eliza Smith, the niece of Lucius Thayer, Jr, a prominent Westfield figure, quickly assumed an active role in the company becoming president of American Whip in 1888. His fellow officers included: Edward B. Gillett, vice-president, Darwin L. Gillett, Treasurer and R.T. Sherman, Secretary

In 1890, Darwin L. Gillett replaced Edward B. Gillett as vice-president and Lewis Parker assumed the position of treasurer. This management team would remain in place until the establishment of United States Whip on Dec 29, 1892.

During its existence the number of employees varied widely from 100 to 400 or more depending upon mergers and the erratic nature of the economy.

United States Whip Company, est. 12/29/1892

The United States Whip Corporation (US Whip) was established Dec 29, 1892, in Portland, Maine. The initial incorporation papers listed the assessed value of the corporation as being $2,200,000.

The creation of U.S. Whip was the culmination of several years of talks and rumors around the creation of a single syndicate to control the whip industry. While the syndicate, as it was called, was supposedly a consolidation of all of the major whip concerns both within Westfield and elsewhere, in reality it became an extension of the former American Whip. The core of U.S. Whips management team were former officers of American Whip. As discussed previously, of the 7 men who signed the original incorporation letters, 4 were former officers and directors of American Whip.

James R. Noble Jr. had the distinction of briefly assuming the presidency of United States Whip at the time of its formation. However, it appears he assumed that role simply to facilitate the initial establishment of the charter and signing of the legal papers. Once the charter was agreed upon, James Noble Jr. having presided as president for two days, elected to remove himself from consideration for the position of president and Lewis R. Norton of American Whip was elected the first formally appointed president. At those same meetings, the size of five members for the board of directors was established.

1893 was a very busy year with as many as twenty companies becoming branches of U. S. Whip in its first year of its existence. Due to the high number of acquisitions, in Sept of 1893 the officers and board of directors voted to increase the size of the board to a maximum of 21 members as the smaller board was deemed insufficient to manage the rapidly growing corporation. With the increased size of the board of directors, as new branches were acquired, many of the former leaders of the more significant acquisitions became directors of U.S. Whip.

Recognizing Lewis Norton didn't have sufficient time to handle the day to day affairs of all of the individual branches, the board of directors appointed Vice- President IRA Miller to be the president of most of the new branches.

The expanded list of officers and directors of the corporation in 1894 with branch company affiliations is shown below.

President	L.R. Norton	American Whip
Vice-Presidents	Ira Miller	American Whip
	E. L. Sanford	Sanford Whip
	F.T. Lay	Lay Whip
	George Pirnie	Massasoit Whip
	R.J. Belt	Wells Whip, Wellsville, Pa.
Clerk	Clarence Hale	Boston, Ma
Secretary	Charles J. Bradley	Sanford Whip
Treasurer	Lewis Parker	American Whip
Directors	John C. Bardwell	Weaver, Bardwell & Humphrey, Moundsville, W. Va.
	R.J. Belt	Wells Whip, Wellsville, Pa.
	C. M. Comstock	C.M. Comstock, Windsor, N.Y.
	W.C. Coggswell	Boston, Ma.
	F. L. Goodnough	Coburn Whip, Windsor, NY
	Charles C. Foster	Boston, Ma.
	W.A. Underwood	Underwood Whip Co., Sydney. O.
	C.A. Weaver	Weaver, Bardwell & Humphrey Mfg. Co., Moundsville, W. Va.
	William H. Milliken	J.H. Milliken & Sons Co., Baltimore, Md.
	Frank Grant	Grant Whip
	David C. Hull	American Whip
	Fred E. Lay	Lay Whip
	Ira Miller	American Whip
	James Noble, Jr.	American Whip
	L.R. Horton	American Whip
	Lewis Parker	American Whip
	George Pirnie	Massasoit Whip
	E.L. Sanford	Sanford Whip, Westfield
	George E Whipple	G. E. Whipple Co.

United States Whip would continue making acquisitions of companies of various sizes for several years, culminating with the acquisition of New England Whip Co. in 1921.

As the industry continue to compress, US Whip would spin off at least 3 business lines in an attempt to diversify. These were Westfield Chemical Co., United States Golf and United States Line Co. Of these divisions, only U. S. Line would survive over the long term.

Dateline of Events

- 1892 - Lewis R. Norton elected first president of US Whip
- 1893 - U.S. Whip acquires over 20 companies in its eighteen months of its existence. (see: Modern Era, 1893 – Present)
- 1897 - Ira Miller elected President succeeding the late L.R. Norton
- 1899 - George E Whipple succeeds Ira Miller as President of the corporation.
- 1908 - Fred L. Parker elected President of U.S. Whip
- 1915 - Westfield Chemical Co., manufacturers of Auto-Wash registered with Westfield Town Clerk, the business appeared in city directories until 1924 after which it ceased being listed.
- 1918 - Acquisition of Independent Whip and its branches
- 1919 - Acquisition of Tipp Whip of Tippecanoe, Oh.
- 1921 - Acquisition of New England Whip and its branches
- 1923 - The U.S. Line Co. division established, manufacturing of fishing lines begins.
- 1927 - U.S. Whip establishes United States Golf Co. division and begins manufacture of golf clubs. which only lasts for 2-3 years.
- 1930's - Production of Whips is terminated.
- 1951 - David H. Comstock succeeds F.L Parker as President
- 1954 - Edward Comstock becomes President of US Whip after death of his brother David H. Comstock
- 1961 - United States Whip Co. sold to Chester Cook Sr., Bradlee Gage and a small group of private investors. Chester Cook becomes President; Bradlee Gage, Vice President.

United States Whip Co., more commonly known by the public as the U. S. Line Co. would remain in Westfield as a manufacturer and distributor of fishing lines and equipment for over 50 years.

Chronological listing of Companies

Included in this section are both Westfield companies and significant firms from other locations which were involved with the evolution of Westfield's Whip industry.

The earliest whip making individuals including Franklin Arthur, Titus Pease, Samuel Lindsey, Joel Farnum and Salmon Phelps have all been previously discussed in the Early Era chapter and have not been re-visited here.

Important notes: Many of the whip companies were located on Elm Street in Westfield. While the author has attempted to establish locations for the various firms, some locations on Elm Street prior to 1887 may appear to be inconsistent with those after 1887. After scrutiny of the Westfield directories it appears the town renumbered Elm Street in 1887. This was likely due to unexpected development of the Street beyond original expectations. Compounding the issue, it also appears that prior to 1887, the odd/even method of numbering sides of the Street wasn't consistent either. One example being C.W. Spencer Whip and Provin Whip Co. While known to have been on Elm Street on opposite sides almost directly across each other, C.W. Spencer was listed as 103 Elm Street, whereas Provin was listed as 155 Elm Street prior to 1887.

Multiple sources were used to establish the dates of operation. As such the dates reflect the earliest and latest dates for which verifiable data was found. However, due to the fact clear records were not always available, these dates should be used as reference points acknowledging that some variance is likely.

Wherever possible the number of employees has been included but many companies did not have employee counts included in the various sources. Most often, the companies reported the number of whips or lashes produced and the corresponding value of their goods. For some of the companies another way of describing their size was the number of traveling salesmen employed and the number of states they sold their goods to. While braiders are sometimes mentioned, these people (usually women) working at home versus in the shops, were often not accounted for. Additionally, in the Federal Census's it appears some firms may have included the outside braiders in their counts while most did not.

1822 - Hiram Hull Whip Co.   (1822 – 1855)
      Location: Franklin St.   *Westfield Standard*, 1851
      Employees: 1850 Fed. Census - 24, (9 males, 15 females)
            1851 *Westfield Standard* article, 15 males, 100 braiders

Hiram Hull's arrival in Westfield has been documented as early as 1810 by some historical accounts and as late as 1821/2 by others. Hiram Hull's death record also states he was 65 when he passed away in 1861. Thus, in 1810, he would have only been 14 years old. The 1821/2 date also appears to be more plausible as Hull's name first appeared in the Hampden County Poll tax records in 1823 when his assessment was $40.00.

After acquiring the rights to use John Thorp's patented braiding machine in 1821, in addition to using the machines for his whip shop, he profited from selling the rights to other Westfield Whip makers for their operations.

A *Westfield Standard* article from Aug. 20, 1851 specifically noted the value of his company at $28,000, significantly down from his 1828 value of $50,000. This was possibly due to his patent rights on the Thorp braiding machine having long since expired and several others had already patented improvements to the machines eliminating his control over the selling of the machines. Also, while it appears his company was worth less than in 1928, this value is for his company not his personal wealth which likely was significantly more.

In 1855, Hull joined with Hiram Harrison and Samuel Dow in the establishment of American Whip.

Hiram Hull also represented Westfield in the state legislature. At the time of his death on Nov. 9, 1861 he was head of the board of Selectmen, a position he had held for 8 years.

1833 – Jasper Rand, J.R. Rand & Son, Rand & Co.,   (1839- 1870)
            Rand, Lewis and Rand

      Location: Elm St. opp. Franklin St., *1857 Atlas of Hampden County*
                        and *1870 Plan of Westfield* map

      Employees: 1850 Fed. Census, 32, (12 males, 20 females)
            1851 *Westfield Standard* article, 20-25 hands with
                        6 females, 40-50 braiders
            1860 Fed. Census, 35, (20 males, 15 females)
            1868 Springfield *Republican* – 80 hands

Jasper Rand started his whip business in approximately 1833. The business operated under the names of under Rand & Son, Rand and Co. and finally Rand, Lewis & Rand until 1870.

Addison C. Rand, son of Jasper held a total of 7 patents issued between 1868 and 1870.

There appears to have been at least a short-term relationship with Derrick N. Goff as evidenced by a Springfield *Republican* article of July 13, 1854 when the two made a gift whip for Edward B. Gillett.

In 1860, rumors circulated that Jasper was abandoning the whip business for that of making women's skirts. Instead, he expanded his business and continued manufacturing both.

A Springfield *Republican* Mar 22, 1865 article describing the whip industry stated his business had been started some 32 years previous (1832) and that his water powered shop with a sufficient number of plaiting machines to enable him to also do plaiting for other manufacturers.

Jasper Rand died Feb 15, 1869 in Westfield. His three surviving sons, Addison C., Jasper R. Jr., and Albert T. would left Westfield for New York City by the early 1870's. In 1871, the brothers founded Rand Drill Company in New Jersey. The Rand brothers later merged with Ingersoll-Sargent Tool Co, forming Ingersoll, Rand & Co. in 1905.

In the final year of their operation, Rand, Lewis and Rand produced a special whip as a gift to Ulysses S Grant just a few months before American Whip purchased the company in early 1870.

The Rand family retained a strong presence in Westfield and were major benefactors of the Westfield Athenaeum. The Jasper Rand Art Gallery is named after the patriarch of the family. Jasper Rand, his sons and many of the family are buried in Pine Hill Cemetery in Westfield.

c. 1833 - **Hiram Harrison Whip Co.** (1833 – 1855)
Location: Main St., per *Westfield Standard* Aug. 1851
Employees: 1850 Census – 115 (40 males, 75 females)
  1851 *Westfield Standard* article. 54 Hands, 'large number of braiders'
  * The 75 females in the 1850 census was likely meant to imply braiders, many of whom worked at home.

Harrison appears to have started his Whip company in approximately 1833-6 when deeds show him acquiring property on the south side of Main Street in the area around what would become Clinton and Taylor Streets. The profile on Samuel Dow includes additional information on those deeds.

Per a *Westfield Standard* article of Aug 20, 1851, Harrison's shop was on Main Street, presumably the future site of American Whip.

Harrison would operate the company until 1855 when he joined Hiram Hull and Samuel Dow establishing American Whip.

In 1865 Hiram Harrison donated the land for the original Westfield Athenaeum on Main Street next to the original American Whip Co. building and is credited as the library's founder.

Hiram Harrison resigned the presidency of American Whip in 1865 for health reasons and died of heart disease on Jan 16, 1869.

1836 – Samuel Dow (1836 – 1855)
        as Dow, Loomis & Co. (1840's - 1853)
        as Dow & Gillett (1854 - 1855)

Location: per 1851 *Westfield Standard*, 2 shops, south end of Elm St.
and 1 on Mechanic St.
Employees: 1850 Federal Census, - 20 males & 50 females
1851 *Westfield Standard*, 30 males, 30 females,
50 braiders

Samuel Dow and Hiram Harrison were listed as purchasing property together in three different deeds during 1836, all on the south side of Main Street. The first of the deeds, dated April 4, 1836, documents Dow and Harrison purchasing a property from Warren Whitman. The location appears to be in the vicinity of Main Street with the final line of the description stating; "Also all the machinery tools and fixtures upon the premises above conveyed." This property was possibly the initial whip shop for Harrison and Dow.

The obituary of George J, Dow in 1902 (Samuel's nephew) also states he was first employed in Samuel's whip shop beginning in 1836.

The *Massachusetts State Directory* of 1850 lists Samuel Dow as a Whip manufacturer, while the 1850 Federal Census lists Dow, Loomis & Co as manufacturing 2,000 doz. whips per year of leather, bone and rattan whips. The *Massachusetts Register of Industry* in 1852 and 1853 also list the firm as Dow, Loomis & Co.

By 1851, it appears Dow's whip factory was located on Elm Street near the stream flowing through the area at that time. A newspaper report of from the *Westfield Newsletter* republished in Boston's *Weekly Messenger* on Nov 23. 1851 describing a flood stated:

" a perfect flood poured down, carrying everything before it, across Elm Street and Mechanics Street, in the vicinity of Johnson's organ factory and Bartlett Streets, emptying itself into Furrows Brook, below Dow's whip factory."

At the time of the formation of American Whip in 1855, the firm was Dow & Gillett. While Samuel Dow joined Hiram Hull & Hiram Harrison to form the American Whip Co., Edward B. Gillett did not join American and established his own firm.

c. 1844 - J. L. Gross & Co. (1844 - 1857)
  Location: Corner of Elm & Franklin St.
  Employees: 1850 Census -   14 males, & 40 females
      1851 *Westfield Standard* article: 21 males & 6 females,
          30 Braiders

Jonah L. Gross established a partnership with Joseph Minor Ely (his son-in-law) in the firm of J. L. Gross & Co. beginning about 1844. Several deeds in the 1840's listing Gross and Ely operating as a company of J.L. Gross & Co. were registered for property on Sandy Mill Road and Meadow Street, in addition to several parcels on Washington Street between Arnold and Franklin Streets.

The firm appears to have initially been very successful. By 1850, according to the Federal Census, they employed over 50 people making it Westfield's 3rd largest whip shop. The census also listed them as producing 24,000 whips and the same number of thongs (lashes) per year at a total value of $20,000. The factory was located on the corner of Franklin and Washington Streets.

However, they appear to have fallen into financial difficulty and had more than one judgement against them in disputes with Hiram Hull, who appears to have been one of their creditors. The exact time of the demise of the company's isn't clear. However, in 1857, in a dispute resulting in an arrest warrant against both men, Hiram Hull purchased much of their property at auction as a result of failure to make payments.

Although the final dispute with Hull was recorded in 1857, it appears Jonah Gross was already in the process of leaving the whip business by 1854. A Westfield *Times News-Letter* article of Aug. 2, 1854 describing the Whip Manufacturers festival, stated the Rev. Jonah L. Gross was "implored to give the blessing to the participants prior to the meal." His death record on Apr 29, 1864 also listed his occupation as minister. (also see: 1857 – Joseph Ely)

1846 - C. W. Spencer & Co. (1846 – 1892)
Location: Franklin St.
Employees: 1860 Fed. Census – Gillett & Spencer, 10 Males, 4 females
1880 Fed. Census - C.W. Spencer, 2 males, 1 female

Charles W. Spencer's earliest known involvement in the whip industry was noted in a 1916 Biographical sketch of his son-in-law, Hiram Harrison Lee. Accounting to that account, Charles Spencer served an apprenticeship to a Mr. Pease at Little River, circa 1831. After terminating his apprenticeship with Pease, he was engaged as a traveling whip salesman for a period of time.

The first documentation having his name associated with a whip shop was the 1860 Federal census which listed Gillett, Spencer & Co. as employing ten males and four females producing 36,000 whips per year at a value of $16,000.

According to various sources, Edward B. Gillett and C. W. Spencer were partners for a couple years, after which he was in business with a Mr. Connor for a short time. 'Mr. Connor' was Jacob Connor, the father of Samuel S. Connor who would establish a bookshop on Elm Street which would become a Westfield landmark for over a century.

On Oct 10, 1861, the Springfield *Republican* published an article stating C.W. Spencer had purchased the whip shop of Gillett, Spencer & Connor. Expected employment was to be about 20 hands manufacturing sword knobs for cavalry purposes and artillery whips for the government.

On March 23, 1864, a *Republican* newspaper article announced a whip to be presented to General H. J. Kilpatrick made by Charles Spencer with no mention of a partner.

The 1872 Westfield City directory listed C.W. Spencer as a whip maker and the 1873 directory specified his location as 103 Elm St. where he would remain until 1886. (Also, see picture of C.W. Spencer shop in the 'Westfield Whip Industry in Pictures' chapter.)

The 1880 Federal Census lists his shop as having only 3 hands implying he was winding down his operation. This is supported by his obituary of Oct 22, 1899 which stated he had retired 7 years previously after over 40 years as a whip maker. His obituary also restated that he initially became involved with whip making at Little River at a young age and that he left whip making for several years before returning to open his own shop in 1846.

1849 – William Provin & Co. (1849 - 1902)
Locations: 102, 105 & 197 Elm St., Provin's Block (1872 – 1902)
Employees: 1850 Fed. Census - 6 males, 8 female
1851 *Westfield Standard* article – 9 males, 20-25 braiders
1860 Fed. Census - 6 males, 6 females
1880 Fed. Census – 9 males, 1 female

William Provin & Co. was founded 1849 by William Provin Sr. William Provin's original factory on Elm St. was slightly south of the factory built in 1874 which later became known as the Provin Block.

City directories beginning in 1874 list William Provin & Co. as being located at 102 Elm Street during its early years, then by 1881 it was listed as 105 Elm Street, subsequently 197 Elm Street by 1887. However, it appears the firm was at the same location in 1881 and 1887 as the numbering of Elm Street appears to have changed twice in the late 1800's. Also known as the Provin block, the building which still survives, is between the railroad trestle on its north side and the former location of the Power building. It is presently the location of a restaurant.

After his father's death on July, 24, 1884, William Provin Jr. operated the company until 1902. In addition to whips, William Provin Jr. was also a dealer in Cigars, Furs, and Skins. William Provin Jr, a civil war veteran, also served two years as a town selectman, three years as a State representative (1886-1887) and two years as a state senator (1891 - 1892) in addition to numerous positions in the private sector.

1850 - Josiah S. Knowles,
Knowles, Josiah S.	(1850 - 1867)
Knowles & Kellogg	(1872 - 1874)
M.D. Knowles & Co.	(1874 - 1876)
Knowles & Hastings	(1877 - 1879)

Location: Mundale, Twine Factory, a.k.a. Ruinsville Mill. (1865)
Granville Rd. (same location) (1872 - 1879)
Employees: 1860 Federal Census – 3 males, 3 females

Josiah Knowles began his business prior to 1850 when he is first listed in the *Massachusetts State Directory*. A newspaper article of 1864 reported that Josiah S. Knowles was retiring form the Whip making business after 39 years in the business but that was either in error or he had a change of heart.

The book, *Mundale, The West Parish of Westfield, Massachusetts* by Eloise Fowler Salmond reported that in 1865, Josiah purchased "The Twine

Factory" in Mundale with his son Milton D. Knowles, Langdon Kellogg, George Peck and Jonathan Hastings.

The firm would undergo several name changes in the next decade. The firm was listed as Knowles & Kellogg in *The Massachusetts Register* in 1872 and 1874. The 1874 Westfield City directory listed it as M.D. Knowles & Co.

Another name change appears to have occurred in 1877 as the 1878 and 1879 city directories list the firm as Knowles and Hastings. Whether all of the firms were Josiah and/or Milton Knowles is not clear. In 1881, Frank Osden bought the mill for use by Osden Whip. (see 1867 - Osden Bros.)

1852 - Hial Holcomb (1852 – 1860)
Location: West Parish / Mundale

Hial Holcomb was reported to have been engaged as a whip maker as early 1834 but was not listed in the 1850 Federal Census Manufacturers of Industry Schedules. He is known to have operated a whip shop in West Parish (now Mundale) by 1852 when a newspaper article reported his factory as having suffered a serious fire in West Parish resulting in a loss of $800-900 worth of manufactured whips. Later information from his obituary and other sources indicate his early shop was primarily a whip lash factory.

By 1860, Hial Holcomb had joined with Solomon Shepard when they were listed in the 1860 Federal Census as whip manufacturers. (see 1860 – Shepard, Holcomb & Co.)

1854 - Coburn Whip Company (I) (1854 - 1872)
    Owen Bros (1872 - 1889)
    Comstock Whip (1889 - 1893)

Location: Windsor, N.Y.
Employees: 1860 Fed. Census – 7 males, 6 females
           1880 Fed. Census – 23 males, 10 females

The Coburn Whip Co of Windsor, New York was actually 2 distinct and different companies. The first existed from 1854 until 1872. The second company, A.W. Coburn & Co., was established less than a year after Adin W. Coburn had sold his original company, became a branch of United States Whip in 1893. (see 1873 - Coburn Whip (II).

When Adin Coburn, a shoemaker, founded the first Coburn Whip in 1854. he recruited Rufus Morey, a young Whip maker from Westfield, to help build the company. Morey was in Windsor, N.Y. by 1858 at the latest, and remained in Windsor for the rest of his life.

At the age of sixty-six Adin Coburn decided to retire, selling his company to Ira Owen who operated the firm as Owen Bros. Whip Co. until he died in 1889. After Owen's demise, the company was taken over by Charles Comstock operating as Comstock Whip until it became a branch of U.S. Whip in 1893.

Charles Comstock left the family and Windsor, N.Y. by 1900 to join one of his sons in Alaska looking for gold. Meanwhile, two of his sons (David and Edward) and their mother would leave Windsor relocating to Westfield. Both brothers went to work for U.S. Whip ultimately becoming the final two presidents of the U.S. Whip corporation before the sale of the United States Line Company, its last surviving business segment, in the 1961.

1854 – Darling, Smith & Co.   (1854 – 1872)
   Location: Elm St.   (1872)
   Employees: 1868 Boston, Commercial Bulletin, 150 hands

The establishment date of 1854 is estimated based on a Mar 29, 1869 Boston *Commercial Bulletin* article stating they had been established 15 years previous. That same article claimed they employed 150 hands, with the bulk of their product made for the Western trade with a large part of it sold from their Hudson, Michigan house.

Darling, Smith & Co. merged with the previously established Westfield Whip Co. in 1872 (see: 1870 – Westfield Whip).

c. 1855 - 1860, James H. Milliken & Sons   (1855 – 1893)
   Location: Baltimore, Md.

James H. Milliken & Sons was founded prior to 1860 in Baltimore Maryland. James H. Milliken was joined by his sons William H. and P. Bryson Milliken in the firm. The company was initially listed as a whip, cane and umbrella maker. James H. Milliken passed away in 1891 in Baltimore, with his sons continuing to run the company.

The company actively participated in the annual whip makers meetings in Westfield during the 1870's and 1880's. Also, R.M. Milliken was listed on the 1874 Annual Whip Makers Ball and Concert announcement as a member of the Honorary Committee for the event.

In 1893, the company became a branch of U.S. Whip with William H. Milliken becoming a director. William H. Milliken was also the holder of 4 whip patents. The company continued operations in Baltimore as a branch until 1904, at which time operations were moved to Westfield. The company was listed as a branch in Westfield City directories until 1923.

1855 - Lester (Leicester) Loomis   (1855 – 1878)
    Location: Mundale, corner of Granville Rd. and Northwest Rd.
    Employees: 1860 Fed. Census 4 males, 10 females

Lester Loomis operated a lash factory in Westfield's Mundale section on the corner of Granville Road and Northwest Road from the late 1850's until 1878. The 1860 census listed his lash business as employing 4 males and 10 females making 5200 dozen lashes at a value of $5,200. Lester Loomis died Jan 4, 1881 at the age of 79 years, 11 months.

1856 – Strong Whip Co.   (1856 - 1907)
    Strong & Woodbury Whip Co.   (1865 - 1894)
    Woodbury Whip Co.   (1894 - 1930)

    Locations: Rochester, New York   (1856 - 1909)
              171 Elm St, Westfield   (1909 - 1921)
              24 Main St.   (1921 – 1930)
    Employees: 1868 - Boston, *Commercial Bulletin* - 50 hands
              1871 - Boston, *Commercial Bulletin* – 70 hands

Strong Whip Co. was the foundation for what eventually became Woodbury Whip in Rochester, N.Y. Myron Strong established his company in 1856 with the firm's name changing to Strong & Woodbury Whip Co. when John Woodbury joined the firm as a partner in 1865.

A *Boston Commercial Journal* article of Aug 8, 1868 that reported Strong & Woodbury employed 50 hands, also stated the company was making 500 dozen whips per month or 72,000 a year. The article also noted business was going so well that their factory was soon to be doubled in size with an expected increase in employment. A subsequent article from the same paper in 1871 stated the number of hands employed had increased to 70.

In 1894, the firm was changed to a stock company under the leadership of J.C. Woodbury and it became Woodbury Whip Company. Woodbury Whip was acquired by New England Whip in July of 1907.

At the time of the acquisition, Woodbury Whip Co. was reported to have a capital value of stock and investments worth $150,000 and being one of the largest whip companies in America. The announcement reported operations were to remain in Rochester. However, in late 1909 the company was moved in its' entirety to Westfield.

Woodbury Whip continued to be listed in the city directories under its own name as a branch until U.S. Whip acquired New England Whip Co. in 1921. After that time, Woodbury Whip was listed in city directories as a branch at 24 Main St. (U.S. Whip) until 1930.

1857 – Ely, Joseph Minor. Sr.
Location: Washington St.

After the demise of J. L. Gross & Co. in the 1850's, Joseph M. Ely continued his career as a whip maker on a smaller scale and passed away on Jun.,14, 1885 at the age of 74 with his occupation still listed as a whip manufacturer.

Joseph Ely was joined in the whip business by two of his sons, Joseph Minor Ely Jr, and James.

His other two sons, Henry and Charles became prominent Westfield lawyers. Joseph Buell Ely, Henry's son and Joseph Minor Ely Sr.'s grandson, also a lawyer, was elected Governor of Massachusetts in 1930, serving two terms from Jan 8, 1931 – Jan 3, 1935.

c. 1860 Van Deusen Bros., (1860-1868) (1876-1878)
Locations: 1860 – Mechanic St.   (1860 - 1870)
1876 – Elm St.
Employees: 1865 – 50, *Springfield Republican,* 3/04/1865

Alonzo Van Deusen formed the firm of Alonzo Van Deusen Whip Co. (a.k.a. Van Deusen bros.) in the early 1860's. Alonzo's factory was on Mechanic Street, near the Bartlett Street intersection. The Map of Hampden County, 1857 shows a 'W Shop' at the location where Alonzo Van Deusen's factory was by the 1860's and the owner isn't noted although it is adjacent to a property owned by 'W. Dewey'. However, the shape of the factory is not the same as pictures of the later Van Deusen story. While it is a hand drawn map, other buildings depicted are historically accurate in the shape drawn. Whether this is an earlier Van Deusen factory or a different whip maker is not clear at this time.

By 1864, the Van Deusens were manufacturing a significant number of whips. It was reported in a Feb 4th newspaper article that their whip factory was manufacturing 360 dozen 'grown up switches' every week.

Alonzo Van Deusen and American Whip appeared to have legal quarrels when a May 7, 1864 newspaper article reported that the local Deputy Marshall had attached the Whip factory of Alonzo Van Deusen in Westfield as a result of a patent infringement claim by Liverus Hull of Charlestown. Liverus (son of Hiram Hull) was running the convict labor in Charlestown prison for American Whip. The claim was for $3000 in damages for a rattan-splitting machine for which Liverus held a patent issued in 1855. Alonzo Van Deusen apparently resolved his differences with American Whip.

On March 22, 1865 a *Springfield Republican*, article about Westfield's whip industry described their factory on Mechanic Street as being 188 feet long, exceedingly well-lit and equipped with a water wheel used for plaiting, turning, stocking and other purposes. The article when on to state they manufactured all kinds of whips including bone, rattan and leather except those known as 'solid leather'. All work was done in the factory with no outside work. The article also noted that they did considerable 'plaiting' for other firms. The plaiting was done exclusively by girls who attended to three and sometimes, but rarely, four plaiting machines at a time. Each machine was capable of plaiting about 6 dozen whips per ten hour working day.

The Van Deusen factory appears to have been equipped with a state of the industry water turbine to power their factory as evidenced by an advertisement of Mar 14, 1866 in the *Springfield Republican*. The advertisement for the Leffel American Double Turbine Water Wheel for which a patent had been issued in 1862, used Van Deusen Whip Co. as a reference customer using their product. Samuel Horton of Westfield was listed as an agent for selling the turbine for the Springfield, Ohio company.

A picture of the original whip shop on Mechanic Street is included in the chapter ' Westfield Whip Industry in Pictures.'

In 1868 Van Deusen Bros. and American Whip merged and Alonzo and his brother Merritt became officers of American Whip. (see 1876 – Van Deusen Bros II)

1860 – Gamaliel King (1855 – 1895)
    Location: Franklin Street   (1855- 1882)
                Elm St. opp. old organ shop   (1882-1895)
    Employees: 1860 Fed. Census – 4 males, 2 Females

    The *Map of Hampden County, 1855* shows a King & Avery whip shop on Franklin street. Gamaliel King and Dexter Avery were known to have a long time association with each other and it appears they had a shop at this location between Madison and Charles Streets until 1872.
    Newspaper reports in 1868 stated his factory on Franklin Street was being expanded to be 44 feet by 20 feet and designed to employ 45 hands and double his production to 100 dozen whips daily. The article noted that the covering (plaiting) for the whips was done in the same building by Dexter Avery on his braiding machines.
    A subsequent article of Jan 30, 1873 reported King as having sold his whip factory for $7000 to Edward Swan and a Mr. Adkins of Southampton. This transaction is also documented in a deed for Jan. 30th having been registered in the Hampden County Registry of Deeds. Edward Swan, in turn, sold the property less than three months later to Eber E. Gridley and Stephen D. Clapp for $8,000. With Eber Gridley having been listed as a mason in city directories, presumably the shop was no longer used in the making of whips. King appears to have immediately purchased the property immediately to the east of his former shop the next day, as that deed dated Jan 31, 1873 listed Swan and Atkins bordering on the west.
    By 1883 his shop was located on Elm Street 'across from the old organ' shop. The 'old organ shop' was presumably the original factory of Johnson Organ on Elm Street. King remained at this location until 1895, the year of his final listing.
    It appears Gamaliel King worked closely with Charles C. Pratt as they held three patents together. Gamaliel had two additional patents in his own name. His patents with Pratt all involved improved methods for covering whips. Of the two patents in his own name, one was for 'loading' stocks (adding weight) and the other for a whalebone replacement.
    Gamaliel King died of heart and kidney problems at the age of 80 on July 24, 1899.

1860 - Shepard, Holcomb & Co.   (1860 - 1875)
    Location: 108 Elm St.   (1874 - 1875)
    Employees: 1860 Fed Census – 5 males, 5 females

Shepard, Holcomb and Co. was a partnership of Solomon Shepard and Hial Holcomb both of whom were listed as individual whip lash makers in the 1850 Federal Census residential listings. Solomon Shepard was also listed in the Products of Industry Schedules of 1850. In the 1860 Federal Census, Products of Industry Schedule, their firm was listed as a whip manufacturer versus simply a lash manufacturer.

The company added Elisha Cook as a partner by 1874 becoming Shepard, Holcomb and Cook. However, that partnership would be short lived due to the death of Solomon Shepard on May 16, 1875, after which the firm became Holcomb & Cook. (see 1875 - Holcomb & Cook)

1864 - Underwood Whip Co. (1864 – 1929)
    Location: Wooster, Ohio (1864 – 1891)
        Sydney Ohio (1891 – 1911)
        Westfield, as branch of U.S. Whip (1911 – 1929)

Underwood Whip was founded in Wooster, Ohio in 1864 by W. A. Underwood. The company was incorporated in 1885 as a stock company with a capital value of $50,000. In 1888, the capital stock value had increased to $60,000.

The city of Wooster, Ohio filed an injunction in 1891 in an attempt to block the company's move to Sydney, Oh. which ultimately failed.

The company was acquired by United States Whip in 1893. While, most of the companies acquired by U.S. Whip moved to or consolidated their operations in Westfield within a short period, Underwood Whip continued operating their whip manufactory in Sydney for almost 14 years. The Sydney factories would not only continue to operate, they actually expanded as they absorbed the work and operations of several branches acquired by U.S. Whip. The Sydney operation was finally moved to Westfield in 1911. The company would continue to be listed as a branch of U.S. Whip in the city directories until 1929.

1865 - Barnes, J. M. (1865 – 1897)
    Location: Thomas St., (1865 – 1875)
        17 Mechanic St. (1875 – 1897)
    Employees: 1880 Fed. Census, 8 (4 male, 4 female)

Jay M. Barnes, born in Feeding Hills, Ma., established his whip and lash factory in Westfield between 1865 and 1870. Jay 'Barns' (sic) was listed in the 1865 Massachusetts State census living in Feeding Hills with an occupation of whip cutter. Jay M. Barnes was in Westfield by the time the 1870 Federal Census was taken..

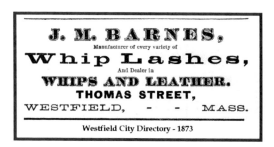

Jay M. Barnes specialized in the manufacture of lashes and ran his business for some 28 years until 1897. Initially, his shop was on Thomas Street then relocating to his residence at 17 Mechanic Street after a fire on Feb 23, 1875 in the Thomas Street building. He passed away at that same location on July 15, 1909.

1865 – Joseph King, King, Whip Co. (1865 – 1898)
    Location: Franklin St. & West Farms
    Employees: 1880 Census - 19 (14 males, 5 females)

Joseph King, a resident of the West Farms section of Westfield was identified as a whip maker by 1865. He later established the office for his company King Whip Co. at 76 Franklin St., relocating to 85 Franklin St. in 1887. Joseph King's home was located in what is now Wyben on Montgomery Road after the intersection of North Road.

While he maintained an office on Franklin Street, newspaper articles at the time of his death reported he still had his whip shop at his residence at West Farms.

Joseph King operated his business for over 35 years until 1898, when he was murdered at his home by his son, Edward. After shooting his father, who was in bed sleeping, Edward also attempted to murder his maiden aunt. He then set fire to the house. As the neighbors were beginning to organize a search for Edward, who was watching from a distance away, he killed himself to evade capture.

1867 - Osden Bros. (1867 – 1874)
Location: Mundale

The Whip companies owned by the Osden family had a tumultuous existence as they involved several different partners and several name changes during its operation.

Osden Brothers Co. was first listed in the *Massachusetts Register 1867*. However, the Osdens were not listed in the city directories until 1874 when they had established a partnership with William Owen as Owen, Osden & Co. The relationship with Owen would fail by 1878, after which they entered a short partnership with George S. Peck, subsequently listed as Peck, Osden & Company from 1878 to 1881.

After the partnership with George S. Peck was dissolved, the Osdens next formed Osden Whip company in 1881. (see 1881 – Osden Whip)

1867 - Schmidt, John C. & Co. (1867 – 1901)
Locations: Corner of Elm & Bartlett (1867-1878)
21 Arnold St. (1878 -1887)
42-48 Arnold St. (1887 – 1901)
Employees: 1880 Fed. Census - 16 (12 males, 4 females)

John C. Schmidt, a native of Germany, migrated to this country at the age of 18, coming to Westfield by 1857 and working for American Whip. After serving in the Civil War in the Mass. 46th Regiment, he began manufacturing whips on his own by 1866-7. Initially, Schmidt was located on the corner of Elm and Bartlett Streets, relocating to 21 Arnold Street by 1878.

In 1887, John C. Schmidt and Robert H. Austin joined together to form J.C. Schmidt & Co. occupying 42-48 Arnold Street. In addition to "manufacturing fancy whips of all kinds", the firm was described as being extensive importers of rattan and whip materials which they supplied to the trade as both raw or finished goods of the highest quality.

By 1891, there were reports circulating that J.C. Schmidt was contemplating returning to Germany due to his failing health. Ultimately, J.C. Schmidt & Co. would be acquired by United States Whip in 1893. Operating as a branch of U.S. Whip, J.C. Schmidt & Co. continued to be listed as operating on Arnold Street until 1901.

A newspaper article of 1897 stated that J.C. Schmidt had retained control of his Arnold Street factory by buying out the lease of U.S. Whip. Schmidt was to reportedly fit it up for manufacturing but would not re-enter the manufacture of whips himself.

J.C. Schmidt died at the age of 65 on Apr 17, 1901 after unexpectedly becoming ill on a trip to New York just 4 days earlier.

1867 – L. H. Beals & Son, aka Bishop & Beals; Bishop, Beals & Lay; L.H. Beals & Co., (1868 – 1915)
    Locations: 201 Elm St., 175 Elm St. (Power Building)
    Employees: 1886 Statistics of Manuf. - 15 - 20

Luther H. Beals began his whip career with the formation of Bishop & Beals in 1867 at 201 Elm Street. In 1871, the company briefly became Bishop, Beals & Lay when Edwin R. Lay was taken in as a partner.

Later in that same year, his son would join the firm. When Wilber Bishop and Edwin Lay departed to establish their own firm of Bishop and Lay (see Bishop & Lay – 1871), the firm's name was changed to L.H. Beals & Son.

Luther Beals was charged with fraud in May of 1897 in connection with his endorsement of $30,000 worth of notes of the Haydenville Manufacturing Company of Northampton which had been assigned by a New York bank. In an obvious move to protect his assets, early in 1897 the whip company had been turned into a corporation with his sons, Charles Beals of Westfield and Prof. Luther H. Beals of Worcester becoming majority owners. His residence in Westfield was also transferred to his sons. After transferring his assets to his sons and wife, L.H. Beal filed for bankruptcy on May 29, 1897. These actions in total caused him to be accused of attempting to defraud the creditors of Haydenville Manufacturing and shielding the whip company and his personal property from being taken over by those creditors. It appears he avoided the charges as the family continued to operate the company.

The company next relocated to 175 Elm Street, occupying 3 floors of the building in 1906, by which time it was called the Power Building.

The Peck & Whipple Whip company had been acquired by US Whip in 1893 as part of the whip consolidation. However, it appears George S. Peck established a relationship with L.H. Beals when, in 1908 the firm registered the name of George S. Peck Whip company as a name or style doing business under their establishment.

On Aug 20.1915 a newspaper account reported rumors that L.H. Beals was going out of business which were denied by Beals. A second article on Sept. 18th stated the company had made assignments to their bank's cashiers. Later that same year, L. H. Beals and Sons would be purchased by New England Whip Co.

1870 - E. B. Light Company (1870 – 1874)
Location: 'old Pochassic' near North Elm St.

The E. B. Light Co. first established prior to 1870, was incorporated Oct 3, 1874 with a capital value of $20,000.

A posting in the Boston *Commercial Bulletin* on June 15, 1872 stated the company was specializing in waterproof whips and lashes making 60 dozen whips per day, having been established some 20 years previous and noted Charles F, Shepard as currently supervising manufacturing.

However, Edward B. Light, born in Perinton, N.Y. a suburb of Rochester, N.Y. in 1842. was too young for him to have established the company by that date. He also served in the Civil War from New York. It is likely that the foundation of the E.B. Light Co. was the Shepard & Co. listed in the *1860 Federal Census, Schedules of Industry.*

Edward B. Light owned 3 patents with two issued in 1872 and another in 1874. The first on Feb. 27. 1872 was an improvement to whip lashes and the second on Dec 17th for a whip lash and snap. The final patent dated Sep. 8. 1874 was for a whip tip ferrule.

A newspaper report of Oct 25, 1972 related that E.B. Light & Co was moving from their current location to the old foundry on the north side of the river after the building had been raised one story and remodeled. Also, the company was listed in city directories as being located at "old Pochassic near North Elm."

Newspaper reports in June of 1875 stated E.B. Light Co. had consolidated with Hampden Whip. However, it appears he failed to formally close down the company as later newspaper articles in 1878 reported the stockholders had petitioned for a dissolution of the company as it had been out of business for 3-4 years.

In 1880, the Federal Census listed him as a Leather Manufacturer in Denver. E.B. Light's masonic membership card from Mt. Moriah Lodge, Westfield lists his residence as Denver Colorado in 1874. He later re-located to California where he remained for the remainder of his life. (see 1875 – Hampden Whip)

1870 – Pratt, Atwater & Co.,   (bef. 1870 – 1873)
   Pratt, Atwater & Goodnow,   (1873 – 1873)
   Pratt, Atwater & Owen   (1873 – 1874)

Employees: 1870 Boston Commercial Bulletin - 40

Pratt, Atwater & Co. was formed by Charles C. Pratt and Leonard Atwater prior to April 1870. In February of 1873, Edward L. Goodnow joined the company and the firm was renamed to Pratt, Atwater & Goodnow.

When William Owen joined the company in 1873 his name was added and Goodnow's dropped. However, the firm was short lived and was dissolved by Jan of 1874. (see 1874 – Owen, Osden & Co.) The company of Pratt, Atwater and Owen was reported to having employed 40 hands in 1870, specializing in what was claimed to be their patented 'elastic rubber-filled whips'. Charles C. Pratt had 2 patents involving the construction and waterproofing of whips just prior to this time and it is likely that is what was being referred to.

In May of 1874, former partner Leonard Atwater would purchase the factory of Pratt, Atwater and Owen. Atwater then re-united with Goodnow forming Hampden Whip (see 1875 – Hampden Whip)

1870 - Westfield Whip Company I (1870-1873)
Location: Elm St.
Employees: 125, per *Springfield Republican* article, 1873

There were two different and distinct companies which operated under the name of Westfield Whip Co.

The initial Westfield Whip Co. was established in approximately 1870 by a group including Lewis R. Sweatland and Charles M. Whipple. In March of 1871, Sweatland and Whipple retired from the company and a new partnership was formed by a group consisting of William O Fletcher, C.M. Darling, James T. Smith and W.B. Weatherbee. Westfield Whip and Darling, Smith & Company merged in November of 1872 continuing operations under the Westfield Whip Co. name

After leaving Westfield Whip, Charles Whipple founded C.M. Whipple Whip Co. (see 1872 – C.M. Whipple & Co.) and Lewis R. Sweatland would establish his own company making Holly Whips.

Westfield Whip relocated to the Manufacturers Co-Operative Building in March of 1873. Business appeared to be very good for the company according to an article in the Springfield Republican on Aug. 2, 1873.

> "The whip business is picking up and the Westfield Whip Company reports an increased manufacture, having produced 30,000 whalebone whips in July. In doing this, they employed 125 persons and their pay-roll foots up to $1000 a week. In addition to the manufacturing, they buy of other firms about

$50,00 worth of lashes and rattan whips yearly. The whips are sold mostly the Western states and on the Pacific coast, though they send large quantities South and East. Six traveling agents are employed by this firm who sell entirely by sample."

However, in spite of a seemingly successful business record, American Whip would acquire Westfield Whip in December of 1873 with James T. Smith leaving the group at that time to begin National Whip Co. (see: 1873 - National Whip)

For information on the second company to operate under the name of Westfield Whip, see: (1884 – Westfield Whip II.)

1872 – C.M. Whipple & Co.   (1872 – 1884)
    Location: Elm St. near Railroad   (1872 – 1878)
             86 Elm St.   (1878 – 1884)
    Employees: 1880 Fed. Census – 13 (10 males, 3 females)

Charles Monroe Whipple, a Westfield native learned the whip making business as a young man working for J.R. Rand. He later became a foreman for Alonzo Van Deusen in the 1860's. He was next associated with the Westfield Whip company until 1872 after which he partnered with William O. Fletcher and Fred P. Couse establishing C.M. Whipple & Company. C.M. Whipple and Co., in turn, merged with George S. Peck in 1884 under the name of Peck & Whipple. (see 1884 – Peck & Whipple).

In addition to his whip business, Charles Whipple served as the chief of the Westfield Fire Department from 1875 until 1887 when he resigned feeling his business commitments prevented him from continuing in that role. After having suffered a stroke some 4 years previous, Charles M. Whipple passed away from a heart attack on July 8, 1908.

1872 - Derrick N. Goff   (1872 – 1888)
    Locations: 106 Elm St.   (1874)
             107 Elm St.   (1878 - 1879)
             168 Elm St.   (1880 - 1886)
             Rear 208 Elm St.   (1887 – 1888)
    Employees: 1880 Fed. Census 6 (4 males, 2 females)

The *Massachusetts Register of Business and Industry* listed Derrick N. Goff, as a Westfield whip manufacturer in both 1872 and 1874. The first listing in the city directories gave the location of his shop in 1874 as 196 Elm St. Goff, a native of Pawlet, Vermont, appears to have been associated with Jasper Rand in 1854 when a newspaper article attributed 'Rand & Goff' as having made a gift of a whip to Edward B. Gillett. No further information on that relationship has been uncovered. However, while Goff was listed as a whip manufacturer in the residential listings of both the 1850 and 1860 Federal Census, there are no entries for him running a business in 'Products of Industry Schedules' for those same census'.

Derrick Goff was listed both under whip manufacturers and whip lash manufacturers in city directories suggesting making lashes were as significant to his business as the manufacturing of complete whips. Derrick N. Goff held one whip patent issued in 1872 for a covering for whip stocks.

Derrick N. Goff died on Sept 25, 1888 at the age of 73. His cause of death was listed as Apoplexy in the Massachusetts vital records. His obituary stated he was the oldest whip maker in Westfield at that time and at the age of 40 he had served as a Massachusetts state legislator.

1872 - George S. Peck & Co.　　　(1872-1877), (1881 - 1884)
　　　　Locations: Franklin St.　　　　　　　(1872)
　　　　　　　Elm St., Horton Bldg., Great River Bridge
　　　　　　　　　　　　　　　　　　　(1873 – 1878)
　　　　136 Elm St.　　　　　　　　　(1879 – 1884)

George S. Peck started his whip shop by 1872 in the factory building of Gamaliel King on Franklin Street. In March of 1973, after King when sold his factory, Peck moved his operations to Samuel Horton's building on Elm Street on the south side of the river. Frank Grant joined the company that same year as a partner.

By 1878, George S. Peck entered into a partnership with the Oden brothers as Peck, Osden & Co. with the company still located in the Horton Bldg. Beginning in 1879 the firm was listed as operating at 136 Elm St. Peck, Osden & Co. was dissolved in 1881 and Peck returned to using the original name of George S. Peck & Co. at that time. After the dissolution of Peck & Osden, the Osden brothers established Osden Whip Co. (see; 1881 – Osden Whip Co.)

From 1881 until 1884, George S. Peck continued operations under his own name. George S. Peck next partnered with Charles Whipple in 1884 as Peck & Whipple Co. located at 141 Elm Street. (see: 1884 – Peck & Whipple Co.)

1872 – Horace Avery   (1872 – 1939)
    Location: 170 Main St.
    Employee: 1880 Fed Census – 4 (2 males, 2 females)

    Horace Avery began making whip lashes at 170 Main Street in 1872. His son Frank H. and then his son Horace continued running the whip lash business until 1939 at the same location.
    In addition to his own whip lash enterprise, Horace Avery was a director of Hampden Whip Co in the 1870's and a stockholder in American Whip at the time of his death.

1873 – Coburn Whip (II)   (1873 – 1893)
    Location: Windsor, N.Y.
    Employees: 30 (1876)

    After retiring briefly in 1872, Adin W. Coburn opened a new whip shop across the street from his old company in late 1873. Within 3 years the new company was reported as employing 30 hands making fifty thousand whips per year. After A.W. Coburn died suddenly in 1877 the company was run briefly by his nephew Llewelyn Coburn who sold it to James G. Fischer. James Fischer, in turn, sold the firm to Richard N. Randall and Franklin Goodenough.
    When U.S. Whip acquired Coburn Whip Co. in 1893, Randall became the manager. Goodenough, who oversaw the operations for U.S. Whip, was a director of the corporation and later ascended to be a vice-president of the corporation. Franklin L Goodnough held at least one whip patent issued in 1887. Although Franklin L. Goodenough was a director and officer in U.S. Whip, he never moved his place of residence from Windsor, N.Y. to Westfield.

1873 - Lay Whip Co. Edwin R. (& Son), (1873 – 1907)
    Locations: Elm St.   (1873)
        rear 107 Elm St.   (1874 -1880)
        Elm St, Provin's Block   (1881 - 1885)
        315 Elm St.   (1887 - 1897)
        360 Elm St.   (1898 - 1899)
        330 Elm St.   (1902 - 1906)

After 1906 listed as a branch at 24 Main (US Whip)

Employees: 1880 Fed. Census   - 17   (12 males, 5 females)
1886 *Mass. Statistics of Manuf.* – 'upwards of 60 hands'

The whip company of Edwin R. Lay underwent several name changes during its existence and is a prime example of how partnerships were formed and dissolved frequently.

The earliest notation in the city directories associated with Edwin Lay was in 1873 under the name of Bishop, Lay & Co. A newspaper article of May 30, 1873 stated Bishop, Lay & Co. had rented Ephraim Crary's manufacturing building on Elm Street which had been formerly occupied by Darling, Smith & Co. However, Wilbur P Bishop would pass away on Nov 21, 1873. After Bishop's passing the firm became Edwin R. Lay Co. and was located in the rear of 107 Elm. The name changed to Edwin R. Lay & Son, in 1878. In 1881 the company was listed as Lay, Barber & Lay. The next change was Lay, Barber & Co. in 1883, then Lay, Van Deusen & Co in 1886.

The name changed once again 1887 when it was incorporated as the Lay Whip Company, located at 315 Elm Street. Lay Whip became a branch of United States Whip in 1893.

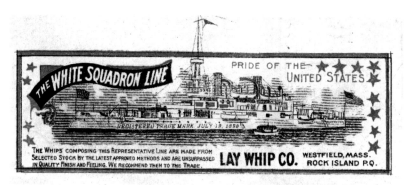

Courtesy Tommy Stanziola

In addition to the Westfield plant, the Lay's had a whip factory at Rock Island, Province of Quebec as can be seen from the above whip label.

The Lay whip factory at 315 Elm Street building became the property of Holy Trinity Church in 1903 and was used as a church until 1910 when the present church was dedicated. After 1903 the church established a school for grades K-8 in the old remodeled factory later adding an addition on Elm Street. The kindergarten class was eliminated in the 1960's.

Edwin Lay had the distinction of having four sons who served in the Civil War from Westfield, two of whom died of their wounds. At the age of 18, James B. Lay was the first Westfield soldier to die in battle. His brother Henry died at the age of "nearly 18 years".

1873 - National Whip Co. (1873 – 1876)
    Location: 1876 Corner Elm and Bartlett St.

    James T. Smith established National Whip after the first Westfield Whip Co. had been acquired by American Whip in 1872. After early success, National Whip was purchased by the Van Deusen Bros in 1876. Less than a year later, James T. Smith unexpectedly died on Jan 24, 1877 of laryngitis and pneumonia, at the age of twenty-nine. (see: 1876 – Van Deusen Bros.)

1874 - Dwight Atwater (1874 – 1881)
    Locations: 103 Elm St. (1874 – 1879)
              41 Washington St. (1879 – 1881)
              San Francisco Ca. (1881 – 1906)
    Employees: 1880 Federal Census - 1

    Dwight M. Atwater began his small whip shop in 1874 at 103 Elm Street, moving to 41 Washington Street by 1879.
    While Dwight Atwater did not have a large whip shop in Westfield, he is linked to a significant historical event. After moving to California in 1881 and successfully building a new whip business, Dwight Atwater lost both his home and business in the San Francisco earthquake/fire disaster of 1906.

1874 – John J. Bohler (1865 - 1897)
    Locations: Atwater Blk, 90-92 Elm St. (1874 – 1879)
                  Elm St., rear Johnson Organ (1880 – 1886)
                 9 N. Elm St., as Bohler Mfg.(1888 – 1889)
                 rear 11 Charles (1892)
                 Allen Ave (1893 - 1897)
    Employees: 1865 Springfield Republican - 28
                   1880 Census – 21

The earliest notation for J.J. Bohler was in 1865, when he was listed in a *Springfield Republican* article on Mar. 22, 1865 as having a whip shop under the name of Bohler & Finney. Their shop was described as having 28 hands manufacturing only 'solid leather' whips, turning out 150 dozen per week. The article also noted that they had several contracts to supply whips to the government for the kind of whip to be used for the artillery service. J.J. Bohler next appears to have had a brief partnership with Frank H. Avery beginning in 1872.

John J. Bohler's first listing as a whip manufacturer occurred in the 1873 Westfield city directory residential listings with his address listed as 51 Franklin St. where he had built a large building for his whip shop the previous year.

In 1880 & 1881 Bohler and his son-in-law Royal Mackintosh were listed as Bohler & Mackintosh. They parted ways by 1882 when Royal Mackintosh left Westfield. After not having been listed in the 1882 city directory, J.J. Bohler's listings for 1883 through 1886 noted his specialty as 'handles'.

1888 saw another change when the firm was noted as a whip snap manufacturer under the name of Bohler Manufacturing Co. He operated under the name of Bohler Manufacturing, making whip snaps for the remainder of his career with a final listing occurring in 1898.

John J. Bohler held at least 6 patents between 1871 and 1888 with his earliest patent for a whip completely made of leather. John J. Bohler passed away at the age of 81 on April 7, 1898 at his home on Allen Ave.

1874 – George T. Moore   (1874 – 1889)
    Locations: 104 Elm St.   (1874 – 1877)
        Elm opp. Franklin   (1878 – 1889)

The G. T. Moore Co. was noted in the city directories as being both a whip manufacturer and a "Plaiter" of whips at 104 Elm Street.

By 1878, Moore had relocated to the Power Building on Elm Street, opposite Franklin Street. In 1880 his city directory listing as whip manufacturer had an added note of 'Toy whips'. Beginning in 1887 his location was at the of rear of 185 Elm, which was possibly the same location as previously but was noted differently due to the address numbers for Elm Street having changed in that year.

George T. Moore would continue to be listed both as a whip manufacturer and a whip 'plaiter' until 1889.

George T. Moore was also the holder of two whip patents both related to attachment improvements for whip snaps.

GEORGE T. MOORE,

WHIP COVERINGS,

Handles, Snaps, and Canes.
Office and Factory in Westfield Power Co.'s Building,
ELM STREET, WESTFIELD, MASS.

Westfeild City Directory - 1886

After 25 years in business, George T. Moore partnered with Leonard Steimer in 1889, establishing Steimer, & Moore Whip Co. (see 1889 – Steimer & Moore).

1875 – Owen, Osden & Co.   (1874 -1878)
Location: 64 Mechanic St.
Employees: 1875 Springfield *Republican* - 50

Following the breakup of Pratt, Atwater & Osden, on Jan 3, 1874, the *Commercial Bulletin* of Boston posted a simple statement as follows:
"Pratt, Atwater, Owen & Co., whip mfgrs, dis; now Owen, Osden & Co.-Wm. H. Owen, E. L. Sanford, F. M. Osden, L. M. Osden"

The company was reported as employing 50 men in their factory which also contained 20 plaiting machines in 1875.
The New York City Directory of 1875 listed William Owen, E.L. Sanford, F.M. Osden and L.M. Osden as doing business from an office at 48 Warren Street, New York City. The Osden's home was listed as Massachusetts, Owen's residence was Brooklyn and Sanford's as Windsor, N.Y. Sanford's being from Windsor is yet another Windsor, N.Y. to Westfield connection. 48 Warren Street was also the address William Owen had been previously using with his former company.
The company, established under the name of Owen, Osden & Co. operated until 1878. After the company was disbanded, the Osden's entered into a partnership with George S. Peck (see: 1878 - Peck & Osden).
William Owen next established his own company of W.H. Owen & Co. (see (1878 – William H. Owen).
Edwin L. Sanford relocated to Westfield establishing Sanford Whip Co. in Westfield in 1880 (see: 1880 – Sanford Whip).

1875 – Holcomb & Cook   (1875 - 1887)
    Location: 108 Elm St.   (1875 - 1878)
             Elm St. cor. of Bartlett St.   (1879 - 1887)
    Employees: 1880 Fed Census   5 males, 2 females

    Holcomb & Cook was established after the death of Solomon Shepard in 1875. Initially located at 108 Elm Street, they relocated to the corner of Bartlett Street by 1879. The firms final listing in the city directories was in 1887.

    The partnership appears to have dissolved by 1888 when Elisha Cook entered into a partnership with his son-in-law Lewis Parker establishing Cook & Parker. (see 1888 – Cook & Parker).

    Following Hial Holcomb's apparent retirement in 1888, he passed away Feb 21, 1900 at the age of 82 years.

1875 - Hampden Whip Co.   (1875 – 1883)
    Location: 92 & 94 Elm St.   (1878)
               Elm opp. Franklin St.   (1879 – 1883)
    Employees: 1880 Fed. Census – 50, (40 males, 10 females)

    In late 1874 Leonard Atwater and E.L. Goodnow formed Atwater, Goodnow & Co. The company was converted into a stock company in January of 1875 under the name of Hampden Whip, admitting several new partners at that time.

    The new partners admitted were reported in a Jan 21th, 1875 *Springfield Republican* article listing the officers of the corporation as; Leonard Atwater, President; C.F. Shepard, Treasurer; E.L. Goodnow, Clerk; and the following board of directors: Leonard Atwater, C.F. Shepherd, E.L. Peck, L.R. Bartlett, Horace W. Avery.

    Over the course of several years, Hampden Whip would expand and absorb additional Westfield firms.
- June of 1875 brought the acquisition of the E.B. Light Company.
- In 1876 Empire Whip and Lash Company merged with Hampden Whip, with the company retaining the Hampden Whip name.
- Van Deusen Bros. would next be absorbed into Hampden Whip in May of 1878.

The company continued to prosper. On August 16, 1878 a newspaper article reported very optimistic results for the Hampden Whip company and with their working nights to keep up with demands. Ultimately, American Whip would purchase Hampden Whip in Jan of 1883.

In addition to American Whip strengthening its dominant role in the industry, the acquisition of Hampden Whip also marked the re-entry of the Van Deusen's into American Whip as prominent members.

1876 – Van Deusen Bros. (II)   (1876 – 1878)
Location: 7-9 Birge Avenue.

Following their departure from American Whip, Alonzo and Mark Van Deusen purchased the machinery and goods of the National Whip Company from James T. Smith in January of 1876. In addition to the equipment, the newspapers articles announcing the acquisition stated the Van Deusen's would also give employment to Smith's employees.

The Van Deusen's operated their latest venture until May of 1878 when the company merged with Hampden Whip. (see: 1874 - Hampden Whip)

1878 - Edmund Cooper   (1878 – 1892)
Locations: 106 Elm St.
(1878)
Blood & Searle's Block   (1879 – 1880)
168 Elm, as Cooper & Hastings   (1881)
164 Elm St.   (1882 – 1885)
164 Elm St., as Cooper & Couse (1886)
rear 198 Elm St.   (1887)
rear 198 Elm St., as Cooper & Austin   (1888)
rear 198 Elm St.   (1889 – 1892)
rear 198 Elm St. (branch)   (1893)

Employees: 1880 Fed Census - 6 (5 males, 1 female)

Edmund Cooper established his firm after a previous partnership with J. B. Fuller was dissolved after less than two years of existence. Edmund Cooper's factory at 106 Elm St suffered severe damage in the 1878 flood which also damaged several other buildings on Elm Street.

Between 1878 and 1888 Edmund Cooper had several different partners as shown above. From 1888 until his final city directory listing in 1893 he was listed under his own name only.

While Edmund Cooper doesn't appear on the list of companies initially absorbed by U.S. Whip in their ledgers, it appears he sold his business to them by 1894. Starting in 1894, he was no longer listed in the city directory business section under whip manufacturers and his residential listing noted him as 'at Amer. Whip'.

Although Edmund Cooper wasn't listed in the business directories as a whip manufacturer after 1893, his death certificate in 1914, when he died at the age of 75, noted his occupation as Whip Manufacturer.

1878 - Peck, Osden & Co.   (1878 – 1881)
    Location: Horton's building, Elm St.   (1878)
             136 Elm St.   (1879 – 1881)

    Employees: 1880 Federal Census – 41 (28 males, 9 females, 4 children & youths)

Following the dissolution of Owen, Osden & Co., George S. Peck and the Osden brothers established Peck, Osden & Co. located in the Horton Building on Elm Street near the Great River bridge.

Much like the short-lived Owen, Osden & Co. the new company would also succumb after only 3 years. In 1881 the company disbanded, with the Osdens forming Osden Whip Co. (see: 1881 - Osden Whip) and George S. Peck re-establishing another company under his own name. (see 1873 – George S. Peck)

1878 - Salmon Ensign   (1878 - 1901)
    Locations: 99 Elm St.   (1878 – 1886)
            188 Elm St.   (1887 – 1888)
            10 Madison St.   (1889 – 1901)
    Employees: 1880 Fed Census – 3

Salmon Ensign, a Westfield native born in 1827, is known to have been engaged in the whip business from an early age. His obituary made note of his overseeing operations at the Charleston State prison. This would have been in the period of 1853-1868 when American Whip had contracts employing prisoners in the manufacture of whips. His first listing under his own name in the Westfield city directories was in 1878 with his last entry in 1901.

The 1880 Federal census lists his shop as a small shop only employing 3 persons. Salmon Ensign's initial shop was at 99 Elm St. and his residence was 6 Madison Ave. For the last 12 years of his shop's operations he ran his business from his residence at 10 Madison Ave.

Salmon Ensign passed away on Dec 5, 1911 at the age of 84, at the home of his daughter Mrs. Samuel S. Connor, the wife of the well-known bookstore owner in Westfield.

1878 - William H. Owen & Co.   (1878 – 1893)
      Locations: 98 Elm St.   (1878 – 1879)
               Elm opp. Franklin, Power Co.   (1880 – 1891)
               187 Elm St.   (1892 – 1893)
      Employees: 1880 Fed. Census - 45 (30 males, 15 females)

William H. Owen formed a company under his own name in 1878 following the dissolution of Owen, Osden & Co. The company was initially located at 98 Elm St. (a.k.a. the Corporate Association Building), By 1880, he was listed as 'Elm opp. Franklin'. From 1880 until 1891 numerous descriptions and addresses were listed in the city directories but further scrutiny shows they were all actually part of the overall Power Company building complex on Elm Street opposite Franklin. During the final 2 years of existence W.H. Owen was located at 187 Elm Street which was the Provin Block.

William Owen resisted being acquired by U.S. Whip in 1893 because he felt the offered value was too low. However, Owen was soon in financial trouble. His factory was attached by Robert F. Parker in November of 1893 with the sheriff taking control of it. The Owen's factory and stock were subsequently auctioned off on Jan 17, 1894 to Merritt Van Deusen on behalf of the First National Bank for $5,300, well below its appraised value of $7,800. Given that the U.S. Whip ledgers indicated they placed a value of $50,000 on the W.H. Owen company, it appears he would have been far better off if he had sold to U.S. Whip when approached.

According to newspaper reports, at the time of the company's failure William H. Owen was estimated as having a net worth anywhere from $75,000 to $150,000, having properties in Brooklyn and Kansas in addition to the Westfield factory.

1879 - Leonard W. Steimer   (1879 - 1882)
      Location: rear 107 Elm St.   (1879 - 1880)
               Blood & Searles Block   (1881 - 1882)

Leonard W. Steimer was born in Brunswick, Germany but grew up in Kingston, R.I. after coming to this country at an early age. After serving in the Civil War from Rhode Island, he came to Westfield in 1869 to work for American Whip. He next worked as a stock room foreman for National Whip for a year. Steimer became a successful salesman for the Edwin R. Lay Whip Co. spending some seven years on the road for the company.

Leonard Steimer established his own whip company in 1879 on Elm Street. After four years, he merged with Frank P. Searle establishing the Steimer & Searle Whip company in 1883, then Steimer and Moore in 1889. His whip career would span almost four decades before he passed away on July 10, 1918.

In addition to his whip career, Steimer was Commander of the Lyon GAR Post, a Past Master of the Mt. Moriah lodge of Mason's and a member of several other associations. (see 1883 – Steimer & Searle, 1889 – Steimer & Moore)

1880 - Sanford Whip (1880 – 1907)
Locations: Mechanic St. (1880-1882)
330 Elm St. (1883 – 1907)

Edwin L. Sanford was born in Windsor, N.Y. His first whip employment was with Coburn Whip in Windsor after having served in the Civil War. He next became a salesman for American Whip operating from their New York office. By 1873 he was associated with Pratt, Atwater & Owen at their New York office, which became Owen, Osden & Co. in 1874.

Following the break-up of Owen, Osden & Co. in 1878, Edwin Sanford relocated to Westfield, establishing Sanford Whip in 1880 in the former Van Deusen Whip building at 64 Mechanic Street. His partners in the new firm included his brother Fred A. Sanford, Charles J. Bradley, Lymon L. Sperry and Lewis H. Lee.

Within 2 years of having been established with an initial employment of about 25, they outgrew the Van Deusen factory on Mechanic Street. A deed dated Oct 19, 1882 has Edwin L. Sanford of Sanford Whip purchasing the tract known as the 'Sackett lot'. That parcel became 330 Elm Street, where he built a new whip factory. The building to be constructed was described as "a three story and basement, brick building, fronting 30 feet on Elm Street, running back 130 feet. The building will have steam power and all modern appliances for whip making."

1885 Trade Post Card, Author's Personal Collection

Sanford Whip was changed from an individual owned company to a corporation in 1888 with the following officers: Edwin L. Sanford, President; Lymon L. Sperry, Vice President; Lewis H. Lee, treasurer; Fred A. Sanford, Clerk and Charles J. Bradley, superintendent. Capital was listed as $110,000.

After the company became a branch of U.S. Whip in 1893, it continued operations at 330 Elm Street, relocating to the U. S. Whip building on Main Street in 1907. In addition to being a director of U.S. Whip, Edwin Sanford was also the manager of the Sanford, Peck & Whipple and Lay branches of the company.

Edwin L. Sanford died at the age of 68 on June 10, 1913.

1881 – Osden Whip Co., Osden, Frank M. (1881-1883), (1884-1897)
Location: Mundale, 'Ruinsville Mill'

The Mundale based Osden's were one of the last factories to operate outside the downtown district in Westfield. Their Granville road factory was known as the 'Ruinsville Mill' due to a legacy of failed businesses which had operated in that location.

Prior to the purchasing the Ruinsville Mill in 181, the Osdens were partners with William Owen in Owen, Osden & Co. A newspaper article at that time reported the firm had decided not to buy the mill because there were fears the workers wouldn't want to leave the downtown district to work in the outlying district of Mundale. There was also speculation that their desire to live the center of Westfield was merely a ploy to negotiate a better lease from their current landlord.

After parting ways with William Owen, the Osden brothers purchased the Ruinsville Mill. From that time on, their firm was listed in city directories as Osden Whip Co, Mundale.

On Dec 13, 1883 a newspaper article announced the company of Osden Whip Company had failed and made an assignment. The company appears to have been dissolved at that time.

Lonzene Osden left Westfield in Feb. 1884, relocating to Rochester N.Y. to become the superintendent of Strong & Woodbury Whip Co. Meanwhile, his brother, Frank Osden, held onto the property and started making whips on his own in the mill. Later listings in the city directories beginning in 1886 were simply Frank M. Osden, Mundale,

Office of **OSDEN WHIP CO.,**
MANUFACTURERS OF
SUPERIOR WHALEBONE WHIPS AND LASHES,
WESTFIELD, MASS.

MR. FRANK M. OSDEN, of our firm, will call upon you on or before *September 5th 1882* and will make it for your interest to examine our Goods before buying elsewhere, as we have many NEW AND ATTRACTIVE STYLES, not made by any other Company.
Telephone and No. 40, Specialties.
Yours Truly,   OSDEN WHIP CO.

Trade Postcard, Authors personal collection

The Osden whip manufactory was destroyed by a fire in 1891 but Frank Osden continued to be listed as running a whip shop in Mundale until a final listing in 1897. Frank Osden joined the Horsewhip company in 1901.

Lonzene Osden returned to Westfield, joining American Whip where he was elected a director in 1888 and was superintendent there for many years thereafter.

1881 - Standard Whip   (1881-1924)
Location: 173 Elm St, rear of Textile Bldg. (1881 - 1910)
287 Elm St   (1911 – 1924)

Standard Whip was established in 1881 by Charles C. Pratt and George C. Phinney. In 1886, Pratt bought out the interest of Phinney who left Westfield for California. C. C. Pratt held at least six whip related patents. Pratt ran the company until his death in 1906 after which his son Edward briefly assumed the presidency. By 1908, James C. McCarthy became the president of the company and remained in that position his death in 1924

The firm was noted as having a specialty of a "Spiral Spring Rawhide" whip. This whip was described as having a top wound with a brass spiral spring wire which kept the rawhide straight and made the whips very elastic and durable. The firm was also described as having a wide range of Rawhides, English Holly and other varieties of whips.

Standard Whip was initially located in the rear of 173 Elm Street. In 1910 the firm moved to 287 Elm Street in the building previously occupied by the Horse Whip Co. Known as the Atwater building, it was purchased in 1914 by Standard Whip from Dr. James R. Atwater. At that time J.C. McCarthy, President and C.J. Rooney, Vice-President were running the firm.

In 1924 the company name was changed to Advanced Whip and Novelty Company and was specializing in small whips and novelty items for fairs. The company was forced to relocate to 350 Elm Street in 1924 after a fire ravaged their building at 287 Elm. After the name was changed to Advanced Whip & Novelty, the company stopped being listed as a whip manufacturer in the city directories as a whip manufacturer.

James C. McCarthy, president of Standard Whip for the previous fifteen plus years, died on Aug 26, 1924 at the age of 66.

1882 – Atwater Manufacturing Co.   (1882 – 1887)

> Location: West Farms, as Oscar Clark   (1876 - 1879)
> West Farms, as Clark, Atwater & Co.   (1880)
> Hosmer Block, as Atwater, Clark & Co. (1881)
> Hosmer Block, as Atwater Mfg. Co.   (1882 - 1884)
> 287 Elm (Atwater Block)   (1885 – 1887)

> Employees: 1880 Fed Census - 7 (6 males, 1 female)

The foundation for Atwater Manufacturing evolved from Oscar Clark's whip shop in West Farms (presently Wyben). Clark's shop was located on the east side of North Road just north of the junction of North and Montgomery Roads.

Oscar Clark established his whip shop by 1876. Leonard Atwater, formerly superintendent of American Whip became a partner in 1880. The company was first listed in the city directory as Clark, Atwater & Co. for one year in 1880, then Atwater, Clark & Co. in 1881.

The company moved from West Farms/Wyben in early 1881 with a change of name to Atwater Manufacturing Co., located in the Hosmer Block. The company relocated to the Atwater block at 287 Elm Street in 1885.

In 1887 Atwater Manufacturing Co. merged with the Chapman & Grant forming Baystate Whip Co. Leonard C. Atwater was elected president of the new company. (see: 1887 – Baystate Whip.)

Prior to moving the whip company to Elm Street in 1881, Oscar Clark sold his West Farms shop to Eunice and Augustus Allen for $2,700 on Nov 20, 1880. In part, the deed described the building as follows:

> "being the premises now occupied by the grantor as a whip shop, together with the whip machinery, engine and boiler in the said building."

The Allen's were first listed in the city directory as whip manufacturers in 1881, operating there until 1890.

1882 - Searle, Frank P., 2nd   (1882 – 1892)

Location:	
rear 106 Elm St.	(1883 – 1884)
5 Hampden St.	(1886)
7 Hampden St.	(1887-1888)
53 Washington cor. Spring St.	(1889-1890)
36 Jefferson St.	(1891-1892)

There were two different men by the name of Frank P. Searle manufacturing whips in Westfield after 1882.

The first was referred in the city directories as "Frank P. Searle, 2nd". It is unclear as to why he was denoted a 'junior' or 'second' as his father's name was Lysander. Frank P. Searle 2nd was born in 1853 and had a whip shop from 1882 until 1892. He operated in several locations either in small shops or his residence until leaving the business in 1892 to become a coal dealer.

The other Frank P. Searle was the man recognized as the owner of Searle Whip Co. and several firms he was a partner in. (See, 1883 - Steimer & Searle, also 1889 - Searle Whip Co.)

The is no clear indication whether the two men were closely related, if at all.

1883 - Steimer, Searle & Co. (1883-1889)
Locations: 103 Elm St, as Leo. W. Steimer (1879)
Blood & Searles Blk, Elm St. (1880-1889)

Employees: 1880 Fed Census (as Steimer) – 5 (4 males, 1 female)

The firm was originally founded in 1879 as the L.W. Steimer Co. Frank P. Searle joined as a partner in 1882 with the company being renamed to Steimer, Searle & Company at that time. Frank P. Searle, who's previous occupation was listed as a bookkeeper, appears to also be primarily a businessman versus a whip making tradesman.

John H. Searle, Frank Searle's father bought an interest in the company in 1883.

The company operate under the original name until Oct. 1889 when Leonard W. Steimer sold his interest in the company. The Searle's then renamed the company to the Searle Whip Company (see 1889 - Searle Whip).

Leonard W. Steimer next partnered with George T. Moore under the name of Steimer & Moore Manufacturing Co. (see 1889 – Steimer & Moore Mfg. Co,)

1883 - Warren Featherbone Company (1883 - 1894)
Location: Three Oaks, Michigan (1883 - 1894)
92 North Elm St. (1894 - 1910)

Warren Featherbone Company was founded in 1883. Although the Warren Featherbone Co was located in Three Oaks, Michigan, it was incorporated in Chicago, Illinois in 1884. The *Daily Illinois State Register* newspaper of Springfield, Illinois announced several new corporations on May 9, 1884 and the incorporation of Warren Featherbone was noted as:

> "The Warren Featherbone Company of Chicago; capital stock, $100,000, incorporators, Edward K. Warren, James H. Hatfield and Benjamin H. Jacobs. "

The company's claim to fame was a material by the name of 'Featherbone'. Earl Kirk Warren received a patent in October of 1883 for Featherbone, a process of using ground up goose and turkey quills as a replacement for whalebone in both whips and women's corsets. The women's corset portion of the business would go on to be significantly more successful than the whip portion of the company.

E. K. Warren was born in Vermont and apparently retained his connection with New England as his son Charles K. attended the Mt. Herman School in Northfield, Ma. His daughter, likewise attended private school in Worcester Massachusetts.

The whip portion of the business became associated with Independent Whip in 1894, although details of that agreement aren't clear. Warren Featherbone Co. retained control of the women's corset portion of the business at their Michigan factory.

In 1894, Charles Clark formerly of Warren Featherbone also became associated with Independent Whip. Charles Clark would later negotiate a termination of the Featherbone agreement with Independent Whip, establishing Featherbone Whip Co. in 1910. (see 1910 – Featherbone Whip)

1884 - Peck & Whipple Co.   (1884 – 1907)
Locations: 141/171/173 Elm St.   (1884 – 1893)
          287 Elm St.   (1894 – 1895)
          360 Elm St.   (1896 – 1906)

George S. Peck and Charles M. Whipple established a partnership as Peck & Whipple Whip Co. in 1884 at 141 Elm Street in the Power Company Building on Elm St. (the address later became 161-177 Elm St.)

They continued their partnership at this location until their company became a branch of United States Whip in 1893. Following the acquisition by U.S. Whip, their operations were moved to 287 Elm St for 2 years. They moved next to 360 Elm St. where they were co-located with Westfield Whip which had also become a branch of US Whip.

Courtesy Tommy Stanziola

After the company was acquired by U.S. Whip in 1893, Charles Whipple became a director of the company. George S. Peck left Westfield moving to Roxbury, Ma. where he died on March 15, 1895

1884 - Westfield Whip Co. II (1884 - 1893)

Locations: 123 Elm St. opp. Franklin (1884 - 1886)
Elm St., South End of Bridge (1886 - 1893)
287 Elm St. (1894 - 1895)
360 Elm St. (1896 – 1906)

After 1906 listed at 24 Main as a branch of US Whip

The second Westfield Whip was formed in Jan. 1884 with the following officers; Reuben Noble, President; George L. Danks, clerk and treasurer; James Noble Jr., H. Winchester and Henry Mullen, Directors. Capital stock for the new corporation was reported as $10,000 in $100 shares.

After two years, at the companies' annual meeting in 1886, the capital stock was raised to $25,000. The new board of officers was comprised of: Louis R. (L. R.) Bartlett, President and Edward L. Goodnow, Treasurer; both of whom became directors along with the following men, Reuben Noble, H. Winchester, James Noble Jr., Henry Mullen and George L Danks. Prior to this, L.R. Norton had held the position of President of American Whip.

In Feb of 1887, Westfield Whip relocated to a new factory at 360 Elm St. in one of the former Johnson & Son Organ Co. buildings at the south end of the Great River Bridge.

On January 2, 1890 L.R. Bartlett declined re-election as president of Westfield Whip. The new officers were: James Noble Jr, President, R.T. Sherman, Treas. (having joined from American Whip) and E.L. Goodnow, Secretary. L.R. Bartlett and Henry Mullen constituted the board of directors along with the aforementioned officers.

A newspaper article of Apr. 21, 1890 reported L. R. Bartlett as having purchased a large orange grove in Florida on a recent trip, where he wanted to retire in the hope of regaining his health. However, Louis R. Bartlett would pass away in Westfield on Aug 27th at his Elm Street home after a long illness.

The company would undergo another change of officers in Dec 1890 when the new slate consisted of: James Knoll Jr, President; Henry Mullen, Vice Pres.; E.L. Goodnow, clerk and treasurer; directors, R.D. Gillett, E.L. Goodnow, C.L. Weller, H Mullen, A.F. Lalley, James Noble Jr., L.H. Dickey.

Westfield Whip became a branch of U.S. Whip in 1893. After the acquisition, the company would continue to be listed as a whip manufacturer in the city directories until 1929.

1885 - A. C. Barnes, & Co.   (1885-1889), (1889-1904)
    Location: Atkins Blk, Elm St.   (1885 - 1890)
          199 Elm St.   (1891 – 1900)
          Power Co. Bldg.,
              Elm cor Meadow   (1901 – 1904)
    Employees: 1886 Mass. Statistics of Manuf. – approx. 40
                                        (male & Female)

    The whip company name of A.C. Barnes & Co. while appearing to have existed from December of 1885 until 1904 was actually several separate companies. Anson C. Barnes also appears to have had a brief partnership with Carlos Chapman in 1883-1884 as Chapman and Barnes before establishing a company in his own name.

    The first company named A.C. Barnes & Co. was organized in 1885 by Anson C. Barnes, Harry M. Gowdy, Henry O. Case and Colling Pomeroy with an aggregate capital of $6,000.00.

    The firm quickly became successful as the publication *Leading Manufacturers and Merchants of Central and Western Massachusetts, 1887*, stated Barnes & Co. had an average production of 6 gross (864) whips and lashes per day. Based on a six-day work week, this would equate to close to 250,000 - 260,000 whips and lashes per year.

    In 1887, after two successful years, Colling Pomeroy sold his interest in the company. At that time, George Pirnie of New York and J. Prout of Brooklyn became partners in the firm. The company, with a value of $40,000, was incorporated as A.C. Barnes & Co. The ownership of the company was a fifty-fifty split in terms of local versus external stock with Barnes, Gowdy and Case owning $20,000 of the stock and Pirnie and Prout holding the other $20,000. Approximately a year later, in December of 1888, A.C. Barnes sold his interest in the company which was then renamed Massasoit Whip Co. (See, 1889 Massasoit Whip).

    Soon after, selling his interest in the first company, A.C. Barnes started another company under his own name, still located at 242 Elm Street. Eugene and Daniel F. Dougherty bought the second A.C. Barnes Co. in 1890. (see 1890 - New England Whip).

    A.C. Barnes started yet another company in his own name that same year at 199 Elm Street. By 1901, the firm was listed as located in the Power Building on the corner of Elm and Meadow Street. There would be a brief partnership with Frank P. Searle creating Woronoco Whip Co. in 1903 which would be dissolved after less than a year of existence. After the dissolution, both Barnes and Searle resumed operations under their original firm names.

A.C. Barnes and Co. ceased operation in 1904 when Anson and his wife relocated to the Boston area.

.

1885 – Chapman & Grant Whip Co.   (1885 – 1887)
    Location: Elm St. opp. Franklin St.

Carlos C. Chapman and Frank Grant established Chapman & Grant Whip Co. in 1885. Their shop was located in the Power Company Building on Elm Street opposite Franklin. (later 161-171 Elm Street).

Chapman & Grant Whip Co. would be become part of the Baystate Whip Co. in 1887. After merging into Baystate, Frank Grant would continue with the new firm for several years. However, C.C. Chapman retired from the whip business in 1888 after less than a year at Baystate Whip. (see 1887 – Baystate Whip)

1886 – Comstock Whip Co.   (1886 – 1892)
    Location: Windsor, New York

Charles M. Comstock started his whip career with Coburn Whip in Windsor, N.Y. In the 1880 Federal Census he was listed as the foreman in a whip factory and lived next door to Rufus Morey, formerly of Westfield and Franklin L. Goodnough. (see: 1855 - Coburn Whip)

Charles Comstock assumed control of Owen Bros. Whip Co after the death of Ira Owen in 1886, renaming it to Comstock Whip Co. Comstock Whip was acquired by U.S. Whip in 1893. Charles M. Comstock held at least 3 Whip patents issued between 1880 and 1888.

Both of C.M. Comstock's sons, David and Edward left Windsor, N.Y. for Westfield and eventually became presidents of U.S. Whip running the firm from 1951-1961. David Comstock's term as president was from 1951 until 1954. Following the death of his brother, Edward assumed the presidency from 1954 until 1961 when U.S. Line Co. was purchased by Chester Cook and Bradlee Gage.

1886 - Pomeroy & Van Deusen   (1886 – 1902)
    Locations: rear 202 Elm St.   (1886 - 1894)
        Allen Power Building   (1895 - 1902)
    Employees: 100 (1902)

Pomeroy & Van Deusen was established in 1886 by John P. Pomeroy and Henry M. Van Deusen. Initially located on Crary Ave, the firm re-located to the S.A. Allen Building on the corner of Meadow and Elm Streets next to the Great River Bridge when expansion of the company required more space in 1895. The partnership was terminated in 1903. At the time of the break-up, it was reported that the firm employed 100 hands.

When the partnership was dissolved, Henry M. Van Deusen assumed all of Pomeroy's interest in the company and the company was renamed H. M. Van Deusen and Co. (see; 1903 – H.M. Van Deusen). The transfer of ownership also included what was known as the Packard Mount Works on Crary Avenue.

1887 – Baystate Whip (1887 – 1923)
Locations: 287 Elm St. (1887 - 1893)
287 Elm St., branch of US Whip (1893 - 1895)
360 Elm St., as a branch (1896 - 1906)
24 Main St. as a branch (1907 - 1923)

On Jan 27, 1888, the *Springfield Republican* reported a planned consolidation of Chapman & Grant and the Atwater Manufacturing Co. companies as a $30,000 stock company for which a charter had been applied for. Leonard C. Atwater, formerly of Atwater Manufacturing, became president of Baystate Whip, while Frank Grant of Chapman & Grant assumed the role of clerk and treasurer. The elected board of directors included: David. H. Atwater, Leonard C. Atwater, Charles R. Fowler, Herbert Lyman, F.F. Van Deusen, Frank Grant. Charles C. Chapman, formerly of Chapman & Grant, became superintendent until he retired at the end of 1888. The company continued operations at 287 Elm St., the location of the former Atwater Manufacturing Co.

After having been acquired by U.S. Whip in 1893, Baystate Whip would continue to be listed in the city directories as operating at 287 Elm Street as a branch until 1895. From 1895 until 1906 the company was located at 360 Elm Street. After that time, the company was listed as a branch at 24 Main Street until 1923.

1888 - Atlantic Whip Company, (1888 – 1898)
Locations: 199 Elm St., Provin's Block (1888 - 1889)
5 Franklin St., Lewis Block (1890)
199 Elm St., Provin's Block (1891 – 1892)

20 Thomas St. (1893 – 1901)

Atlantic Whip was established in January of 1888, by Newton S. Barnes, Wolcott Daniels and Henry O. Brigham. Barnes and Daniels were the whip makers, with Brigham a bookkeeper. Brigham would leave by 1895 to become bookkeeper for Cargill & Cook Co.

Atlantic Whip operated until 1901 with its last listing in the city directories at that time. The company appears to have been dissolved at that time as Wolcott Daniels was listed in the business listings under his own name for one year in 1902. Meanwhile, in 1902 Newton Barnes was listed in the residential listings as a whip maker but did not have a listing under the business listings.

1888 – Cook & Parker Whip Co. (1888 – 1901)
Location: 231 Elm St., corner of Bartlett.

Cook and Parker was established in 1885 following the retirement of Hial Holcomb, Elijah Cook's former partner. The new partnership of Elijah Cook and Lewis Parker continued operations at 231 Elm Street on the corner of Bartlett Street. Lewis Parker left the firm in 1890 to join the American Whip Co. as treasurer, assuming the same position when U.S. Whip was established. While the firm was listed as operating at their former location, they were a branch of U.S. Whip having been acquired in 1893.

Elisha Cook passed away on June 26, 1898, although the company continued operating under the name of Cook & Parker until 1901.

1888 - Cargill, Cook & Co. (1888 - 1905)
Location: 210/212 Elm St. (1888 - 1893)
177 Elm St. (1894 – 1905)

Cargill, Cook & Co. was originally established in Southfield, Ma. in 1884 as Barber, Cargill & Cook and operated there until 1888 when Wilbur G. Cargill and Arthur J. Cook moved the firm to Westfield and changed the name to Cargill, Cook & Co. Wilbur Cargill and Arthur J. Cook became the sole proprietors in 1891. By 1897, they occupied two floors of the Power Company Building at 177 Elm St.

Cargill, a native of Tioga county New York headed up the sales side of the company, while Cook, a native of Southfield, Ma. was the whip maker in charge of the manufacturing side of the organization. In 1905, A. J. Cook sold his interest in the firm to Harvey J. Cleveland and formed the A.J. Cook Whip Co. (see 1905 – A.J. Cook). Following the exit of A. J. Cook and Harvey J. Cleveland having joined the company, the firm became Cargill, Cleveland and Co. (see 1905 - Cargill, Cleveland & Co.)

1889 - Massasoit Whip Company   (1889-1923)
        Locations: 352 Elm   (1889)
                   360 Elm St.   (1890 – 1894)
                   330 Elm, as a branch   (1895 – 1898)
                   360 Elm, as a branch   (1902 – 1906)

       After 1906, listed as a branch at 24 Main (U.S. Whip)

    The Massasoit Whip Co. was established in early 1889 after A.C. Barnes sold his interest in the original A.C. Barnes & Co. in December of 1888. At that time George Pirnie, who was Vice-President of the original company was appointed president.
    Massasoit Whip was initially located at 352 Elm Street, moving to 360 Elm by 1890. Massasoit was absorbed into the U.S. Whip syndicate in 1893 but continued to be listed at 330 or 360 Elm Street as a branch until 1906. After 1906, it was listed as a branch at 24 Main St. (U.S. Whip's address) until 1923

Courtesy Tommy Stanziola

    The two patent dates on the above whip label are the issue dates for two patents assigned to George Pirnie who was identified as living in Nyack N.Y. at the time of their issue.

1889 – Searle Whip Company (1889-1905)
        Locations: 226 Elm St. (1889-1893)
        Allen Power Bldg., Great River Bridge
        (1893-1904)

    Searle Whip Co. was created in 1889 after the dissolution of Steimer, Searle & Co. Searle Whip continued operations at 226 Elm Street in the same building.
    By 1894 Searle Whip had relocated to the Allen Power Building on the corner of Elm Street and Meadow Street next to the south end of the Great River Bridge.
    An accounting of Searle Whip Co. in the Westfield *Times and Newsletter, Special Trade Edition* of Oct 6, 1897 described their company as occupying their large factory on the bank of the river and making all parts of their whip with the exception of the stock which was made under contract.
    The article in the Times Newsletter also described their whips as:

> "Their trademarks which have made their goods staple in any stock are 'Woronoco", "Amazon", "Vulcanized' costing anywhere from 50 cents a dozen to sixty dollars, and for special orders they furnish anything desired."

    In 1903 Frank P. Searle dissolved his partnership with his father James H. Searle, a long-time investor in the firm. That same year, Frank P. Searle and A.C. Barnes formed a partnership establishing Woronoco Whip Company in Jan of 1903. However, the partnership would be short-lived as Woronoco Whip Co was dissolved in 1904 after having only been in business for slightly over a year. Searle and Barnes returned to running their individual companies under their original names at that time.
    New England Whip acquired Searle Whip, in October 1904 to be run as a branch of the lager company, retaining Frank P. Searle as general manager of his former firm. (See 1890 – New England Whip)

1889 - Steimer & Moore Mfg., aka Steimer & Moore Whip Co. (1889 - 1918)
        Locations: 199 Elm St. (1889 – 1891)
                 10 Birge Ave. (1991 – 1918)

    After selling his interest in Steimer & Searle Whip Co., Leonard W. Steimer partnered with George T. Moore establishing a new firm under the name of Steimer & Moore Manufacturing. Officers of the new company were: L. W. Steimer, President; Geo. T. Moore, Vice President and E.A. Kenyon, secretary and treasurer.

Ad from *Western New England*, Feb 1911

The new company was initially located at 199 Elm Street, also known as the Provin Building. By 1891, Steimer & Moore had relocated to 10 Birge Ave. where it would operate until it became a branch of United States Whip in 1918.

The *1906 Souvenir of Westfield* listed the officers of the corporation as Leonard Steimer, President; Thomas Horwood, Vice-President and J.H. Lounsbury, Treasurer. J.H. Lounsbury, a machinist owned the 10 and 12 Birge Ave. properties and ran his own machinery business as J.H. Lounsbury at 12 Birge Ave from 1891-1907. John H. Lounsbury passed away Apr 26, 1907 with Steimer & Moore purchasing their building from his estate in Mar 11, 1909.

During their partnership, Leonard W. Steimer and George T. Moore would share one whip patent in 1894 for an improved whip core. George T. Moore had previously obtained another whip patent in 1887 for an improvement to whip snaps.

George T. Moore appears to have left active involvement in the company by 1902 having relocated to Everett, Ma. where he was listed as a machinist in the city directories.

Leonard Steimer passed away on July 9, 1918. His obituary stated his factory was still at 10 Birge Avenue but he had not been actively involved in the company for several years. The company became a branch of U.S. Whip shortly before his death with the 1918 city directory listing it as a branch of US Whip at that time.

1889 - Tipp Whip Company (1889 - 1919)
    Location: Tippecanoe, Oh. (1889 - 1919)
    24 Main St., as a branch (1919 – 1924)
    Employees: 1909 - 35

Tipp Whip was founded in 1889 in Tippecanoe, Ohio by Alba Lloyd Harshbarger and Frank Davis. In 1909 it was described in newspaper accounts as a buggy whip maker employing 35 workmen.

Tipp Whip was acquired by U.S. Whip in Feb 1919 and was as a branch until 1924. This acquisition was the final acquisition by U.S. Whip of whip companies located external to Westfield.

1890 - New England Whip Co.   (1890 – 1921)
Locations: 242 Elm St.   (1890 - 1893)
Cherry St. cor. Mechanic St.,   (1893 - 1900)
Power Bldg., 169-173 Elm St.   (1900 - 1921)

New England Whip was formed in 1890 by Daniel and Eugene Doherty. Eugene Doherty had previously been listed as making whip stocks in the Power Company Building in 1889. Daniel F. Doherty, a clerk in the Post Office for seven years and in charge of the money order department, left that position in December of 1892 to join his brother running the company.

The company's first location was 242 Elm Street and it operated there from 1890 until 1893 when it relocated to the Ensign Box factory on the corner of Mechanic and Cherry Streets (presently 22 Cherry St.). By 1900, the company had outgrown its space in the Ensign Building, and began leasing space in the Textile Mfg. Building (a.k.a. Power Building) at 169 - 173 Elm Street, where it would remain until being purchased by United States Whip in 1921.

In an interesting turn of events, the company underwent a change in leadership in 1897 when the Yukon Gold rush beckoned. J.E. Perrins resigned the presidency at that time to join a group of 15 people in search of their fortune in the Canadian Northwest Klondike territory.

In 1904, Searle Whip, founded in 1889, was purchased to be run as a branch of New England Whip with former owner Frank P. Searle being retained as superintendent. The company continued to prosper prompting the Power Company to enlarge its building in 1906. The company's growth was noted in the *1906 Souvenir of Westfield* which described New England Whip as being the 2nd largest Whip Company in the world (after U.S. Whip) and doing a business of $500,000 a year.

New England whip continued expanding with the acquisition of Woodbury Whip Co. of Rochester, N.Y. in 1907. Initial reports were that Woodbury Whip would continue operation in Rochester. However, in 1909 the branch was relocated to Westfield closing its Rochester plant.

A newspaper article on June 25, 1915 speculated in length about a proposed merger of New England Whip and Independent Whip. The merger would reportedly result in New England Whip surpassing US Whip as the largest Whip firm in the world. However, the merger never came to fruition and Independent Whip was acquired by U.S. Whip in 1918.

Ultimately, on March 21, 1921 New England Whip was acquired by U.S. Whip. The merger of the two large whip firms was the last merger of significance for the whip industry in Westfield.

1894 - American Holly Whip Company, (1894-1930)
    Locations: S.A. Allen Bldg., Great River Br. (1894 - 1898)
          rear 208 Elm St.   (1898 - 1899)
          90 Orange St.   (1900 - 1910)
          10 Lincoln St.,   (1911 – 1930)

Established about 1894 in the S.A. Allen Power Building, American Holly Whip was relocated to the rear of 202 Elm by 1898. Its next location was 90 Orange Street from 1900 until 1910 with their final operation at 11 Lincoln St. in 1930. American Holly Whip Co. was a small manufacturer specializing in whips made with English Holly wood handles.

AMERICAN HOLLY WHIP COMPANY,
Manufacturers of all kinds of
Knotted and Carved Whips,
Whip Handles, Crop Sticks and Riding Whips.
OAK AND HICKORY STOCKS.
Always a Large Assortment on Hand.
H. W. HAMMERSLEY, Proprietor.
Allen's Power Building, corner Elm and Meadow Streets,
Westfield, Mass.

                                            Westfield City Directory - 1895

1894 -Independent Whip   (1894-1918)
    Locations: 187 Elm St.   (1894 - 1902)
          92 North Elm St.   (1902 - 1918)
    Employees: Approx. 150

Independent Whip Co. was established in February of 1894 with an initial capital stock of $45,000. The company purchased the Owen Whip factory at

187 Elm Street as its initial place of business. Independent Whip built a new factory on North Elm Street in late 1902 and occupied it by Jan 1, 1903.

By 1916, Continental Whip, Consolidated Whip, Cowles-Horan, and National Whip were all listed as located at 92 North Elm Street along with Independent Whip. While the city directories only designated National Whip as a branch, it appears all were assets of Independent Whip as they were all included in the package when United States Whip purchased Independent Whip on Mar. 12, 1918.

When Independent Whip was purchased, President Edward Cowles became a director of U.S. Whip. The newspaper articles announcing the buy-out stated that Independent Whip would operate in its current location for the present.

The North Elm Street building was sold to the Federal Corporation on Aug. 1, 1919. In 1922 the building became the home of Old Colony Envelope Company. Old Colony Envelope operated there for the next 75 years before moving to Turnpike Industrial Road in 1997.

1894 – National Manufacturing Co. (1894 – 1920)
Location: 7-9 Birge Avenue (1894 – 1900)
224 Elm St. (1905 – 1920)

National Manufacturing Co. was first listed in the Westfield city directories in 1894 at 7-9 Birge Ave. The company appears to be a continuation of the firm listed under the name of J. E. Mesick starting in 1889 at the same location. Beginning in 1894, when National Manufacturing was listed in the business section, James Mesick's residential listing had him working at National Manufacturing. Whether Mesick sold the business, took on partners or simply renamed the firm isn't clear but he obviously was still actively engaged.

Both James E. Mesick's original business and that of National Manufacturing were identified as being whip lash manufacturers. From 1900 until 1905 the firm is not listed in the city directories, likewise, James Mesick's residential listing doesn't note anything about his being at National Mfg.

The firm reappeared in the directory listings in 1906 at a new location of 224 Elm Street with James E. Mesick listed as manager. James Mesick continued as manager of the company until his sudden death of a heart attack at his home the afternoon of Sept 21, 1915.

National Manufacturing's final listing in the city directory was in 1920.

1901- Horse Whip Company (1901 - 1933)
    Locations: Thomas St. (1901)
              287 Elm St., (1902 - 1908)
              Rear of 273 Elm St., (1909 - 1933)
    Employees: 40-50 – *Springfield Republican*, 1902

The Horse Whip Company was formed in Aug. 1901 with the initial officers being comprised of President, Frank O. Hudson (formerly of Independent Whip); vice president, C.W. Vayo of Rochester, New York; Clerk, W.W. Sterling of Elkhart, Indiana; Treasurer, Marcus M Broga.

Marcus Broga was formerly head of Broga & Noble which was absorbed into the new company. Initially, the company operated in Broga & Noble's former factory on Thomas Street for a short period and relocated to the former Baystate Whip factory at 287 Elm St. after it was remodeled.

The company's specialty was a whip by the name of 'ZebuAzo' which was promoted as a more flexible and durable replacement to Whalebone. ZebuAzo was one of many innovations by various companies in an attempt to replace whalebone as the material of choice for high quality whips.

The company experienced early success with their workforce growing to 40-50 by February of 1902 when a new engine of 25 horsepower and a generator for lighting the factory were installed.

However, by the fall of 1903 a split amongst the management occurred resulting in Frank Hudson and W.W. Sterling leaving and selling their stock to Broga and Vayo. It is apparent the split was not amicable as a committee of independent men where appointed to appraise the company to set the price for the buyout of the partners. The committee consisted of Charles J. Bradley (Manager, Independent Whip), Charles H. Beals (Secretary & Treasurer, Beals Whip), and H.M. Van Deusen (President, Van Deusen Whip).

Horse Whip ceased operations in 1933.

1903 – H.M. Van Deusen Whip (1903 - 1930)
    Locations: Allen Power Bldg., Great River Br. (1902 - 1917)
              42-46 Arnold St. (1917 - 1930)

Henry Van Deusen, born in Hillsdale, N.Y., began his whip career in Southfield Ma. After learning the whip trade as a young man, while still in Southfield he became a partner in Hawley & Van Deusen Whip Co. in 1872. After moving to Westfield in 1880, Henry Van Deusen purchased goods from Edwin Lay & Sons and traveled across the country building up a trade.

He entered into partnership with Lay in 1885 as Lay, Van Deusen & Co. which lasted for almost two years, at which time he left the firm.

Henry M. Van Deusen and John P. Pomeroy then established Pomeroy & Van Deusen Whip Co. in 1886 at the rear of 202 Elm Street. In 1900, they relocated to the S.A. Allen building on Elm Street near the Great River Bridge. The partnership lasted until 1902 when John Pomeroy sold his interest in the company to his partner. The former firm was dissolved and a new company established under the name of H. M. Van Deusen Co. Over time the building became more well known as the Van Deusen Building. The Van Deusens also leased space to the Searle Whip company and others in the large factory.

In 1917 a new plant was built on Arnold Street which in later years would become the headquarters for Stanley Home Products Inc. By 1920, the building was occupied by both H.M. Van Deusen Whip and the Planet Company which the Van Deusen's had purchased several years previously.

The former S.A. Allen building which had become known as the Van Deusen Building was seriously damaged in the hurricane of 1927 and would succumb to the flood of 1938 after which the remains were demolished.

Henry M. Van Deusen stayed active in the company until he passed away at the age of 79 on March 27, 1930. At the time of his death he was Westfield's largest taxpayer, owner of the Van Deusen Inn, Central Hotel, and the Sunnyside Ranch in Southwick. He was a member of many social organizations, a former vice-president of both the First National and Westfield Savings Banks for many years and also served in the state legislature in 1896.

A newspaper article on Oct 18, 1930 announced the company had ceased operation, the machinery was to be sold and the property was to be disposed of in order to settle the estate. (also see: 1906 - Spencer-Martin Whip Co.)

1905 - A.J. Cook Whip Co.   (1905 - 1912)

Location: Cherry St. near Mechanic St.   (1905 – 1912)

Employees: per 1906 Springfield *Republican* - 45

After a total of twenty years in partnership with W.G. Cargill originating at Southfield, Mass, Arthur (A.J.) Cook left Cook & Cargill Co. in 1905. A. J. Cook then started his own firm in the old Ensign Box factory on the corner of Cherry & Mechanic Streets.

When the new firm was established, Cook expected to employ 25 to 30 hands. By Jan 18, 1906, a newspaper article reported that business was going so well that the capital of the firm had raised from $30,000 to $45,000 and the number of hands employed had increased to 45.

In Jan of 1907, Cargill & Cleveland filed a complaint against A.J. Cook for using the label known as the "Early Bird", which reached a hearing in the state Supreme Court. Ultimately, the two firms reached a compromise resulting in the dismissal of the complaint.

Howard J. Noble and Arthur J. Cook registered the company name of Reliance Whip with the Westfield town clerk on Jan 18,1908. A.J. Cook Whip continued to be listed in the city directories until 1912 after which A.J. Cook left the whip business and started a real estate and insurance business on Elm Street.

Meanwhile, for 1913 only, Reliance Whip was listed at the same location before it too passed from existence.

1905 - Cargill, Cleveland & Co.   (1923 – 1951)
   Locations: 177 Elm St.   (1905 – 1922)
              360 Elm St.   (1923 – 1951)

Following the departure of A.J. Cook from Cargill, Cook & Co. in 1905, Harvey J. Cleveland became a partner and the firm became Cargill, Cleveland and Co.

Initially Cargill, Cleveland & Co. was located in the Power Building at 177 Elm Street. In 1923 the company bought the building at 360 Elm Street from the Rogers Silver Co. which had resided in the building for several years after acquiring it from the Massasoit Whip Co.

The Atlantic Whip Co. name was registered by Cargill & Cleveland with the Westfield town clerk in Dec 1907. Also, Rawhide Whip was registered as a business name in 1912.

One of Cargill, Cleveland and Company's claims was the vast number of whip styles and customization they performed. A sales catalog from the 1930's illustrating over 150 whips made by Cargill and Cleveland has whips of every type and description. The catalog has a notation on its last page stating;

> "The above is only a small sample of the lines which we manufacture. We are pleased to state that we can furnish you with anything that is made in the whip line, as we manufacture something like 800-1000 styles."

Beginning in 1923 Cargill, Cleveland & Co. made whips for the Barry Whip Co. While the relationship was initially a manufacturing contract to produce whips for Barry Whip Co., over time Maurice Barry Whip would become integrated with Cargill & Cleveland with Maurice Barry primarily involved as a salesman. Maurice Barry became the president of the company after the deaths of Wilbur Cargill in 1933 and Harvey J. Cleveland in 1935.

Maurice Barry remained president until his passing on Mar 4, 1940. Following Maurice Barry's death, his sister Genevieve L. Barry who had previously lived on Long Island, assumed control of the company serving as president until the company was purchased by Harold J. Martin of Westfield Whip Manufacturing Co. in 1951. (see 1946 - Westfield Whip Manufacturing)

1906 – Spencer-Martin Whip Co. (1906 – 1916)

Locations: 298 Elm St. (1906 - 1909)
198 Elm St, as a branch (1909 - 1916)

The whip company Spencer-Martin first appears in the 1906 city directory located at 298 Elm St. In 1908 Henry Van Deusen filed a notice with the Westfield town clerk that he and Edward P. Turner of Maine were co-partners of Spencer-Martin Whip Co. While no further details were found, it appears that Spencer-Martin was named for Henry Van Deusen's son, Spencer Martin Van Deusen, although he would have only been 15 at the time of its being established.

Spencer M. Van Deusen was listed in the city directories as associated 'with the H.M. Van Deusen Whip Co.' beginning in 1909. Also, beginning in 1910 Spencer-Martin Co. began being listed as a 'branch'. Spencer-Martin Whip Co.'s last listing in the city directories was in 1916.

1910 – Featherbone Whip Company (1910 -1922)

Charles H. Clark, born in Rochester, N.Y. in 1854, would become known as "Mr. Featherbone" locally in Westfield.

Charles H. Clark, was originally associated with E.K. Warren Featherbone in Three Oaks, Michigan and some later accounts claimed be invented the Featherbone whip. However, while he was known to have worked for E.K. Warren, his name was not on the original patent nor was he named as one of the original incorporators of the E.K. Warren Co. in 1884. Newspaper reports credit him as being a salesman in Chicago at the time of E.K. Warren's invention of Featherbone and his going to Three Oaks to help build the whip side of the company.

Charles H. Clark received a patent in 1917 for a method of improved construction of the lash loop which was one of the parts having proved to be most vulnerable to failure. Specifically, the process consisting of a bonding of the loop to the core of the whip versus simply being braided. The loop itself involved the use of feather quills making it an extension of the use of Featherbone as a whalebone replacement to the core itself.

Charles H. Clark operated Featherbone Whip until 1922 when he committed suicide in Atlantic City. It was reported he had been battling depression for several months and was vacationing with his wife in Atlantic City at the time of his death.

1914 – Barry Whip Co.   (1914-1921, 1923 -1938)
Locations: 171 Elm St   (1914 – 1921)
360 Elm St.   (1923 – 1938)

Barry Whip Company wasn't actually a whip manufacturer, the company grew out of Maurice Barry's having been a lead salesman for New England Whip. Barry Whip Co. was formed as a trade name and marketed as it's own company but the whips were made by New England Whip. When New England Whip was purchased by U.S. Whip in 1921, the assets of Barry Whip were part of the package.

Following the acquisition, Maurice Barry registered the Barry Whip Co. name in Westfield which appears to have been challenged by U.S. Whip. Barry then filed a suit against U.S. Whip claiming his interests had been improperly sold out from under him without his knowledge or consent.

In 1923, Barry succeeded in having the company name restored to him. Instead of establishing his own manufacturing factory, he contracted with Cargill & Cleveland to make the whips which he marketed under the Barry Whip name. Barry Whip Co. became a sales distributor/branch within Cargill & Cleveland with Maurice Barry taking a more active role in the full company. Barry would go onto become president of the company following the deaths of Wilbur Cargill and Harvey Cleveland. (see 1905 - Cargill, Cleveland)

1946 - Westfield Whip Manufacturing Co. (1946 – present)
Locations: 44 Court St.,   (1946 – 1951)
360 Elm St.,   (1951 – present)

The final significant whip company to be established in Westfield is Westfield Whip Manufacturing Co. The company was formed in 1946 by Harold Martin who would later become mayor of Westfield. The company moved into the former Cargill, Cleveland & Co. building at 360 Elm Street in 1951 after Martin acquired the assets of Cargill, Cleveland & Co.

The company has remained under the ownership of the Martin family operated by Harold Martin's daughter, Carol Martin and is the last active whip company in Westfield. Having operated for 72 years, it also holds the distinction as the longest running whip company to have operated under a single name.

While the company has evolved with new methods and materials as the industry has changed, the factory has many artifacts and machines which harken back to the early days of the industry.

The Westfield Whip Manufacturing Co. building has been registered as a National Historical site. As of the writing of this book the factory is in the process of renovations to open it as a historic museum.

1962 – Grudowski, Edward,   (1962 – 1967)
Location: rear 34 Meadow St.

Edward Grudowsky operated Great American Leather Products manufacturing a small number of whips from 1962-1967. Grudowski's shop was at the rear of 34 Meadow Street. Great American Leather relocated to the Crescent Mills section of Russell by 1967.

Summary

As 2018 and the completion of this book draws to a close, it is important to revisit the importance of the whip industry to Westfield Massachusetts.

It cannot be overstated that without the whip industry, Westfield, Massachusetts would not be the city it is today. As stated earlier, in the mid-late 1800's the whip industry was fifty percent or more of Westfield's overall economy. As such, it provided the financial base to enable other industries to thrive.

The town continued to prosper with the addition of several new industries in the mid-1800's including the cigar and tobacco growing industry, H.B. Smith & Co. and Jessup & Laflin Paper Co. These businesses were followed later in the century by companies such as Warren Thread Works, Foster Machine Co., Springdale Paper Co., Crane Brothers Paper Co. and Lozier Manufacturing which later became Columbia Manufacturing.

The twentieth century brought additional changes with the addition of Strathmore Paper Company, Old Colony Envelope Co., Stevens Paper Co. (from Crane), and many others. These industries would be joined by a growing and thriving industry of precision machine shops. As these industries evolved, it is also significant that Westfield retained much of its agricultural base contributing to the diversity of the community and creating a balance lacking in many towns and cities of that era.

While most of the aforementioned industries have disappeared from Westfield's landscape, they illustrate how the city has been in a state of transition for over 150 years. The ability to evolve from one industry to another has enabled Westfield to avoid the severe economic decay encountered by many cities and towns in the New England region whose base industries such as textiles, paper manufacturing, shoes, etc. declined or transferred to other locations.

Since 1951, the Westfield Whip Manufacturing Co. has been the sole whip manufacturer sustaining Westfield's link to its past. Westfield is also fortunate to have the resources in the archives of the Westfield Athenaeum and the whip museum currently under development to ensure our connection to the whip industry is not forgotten.

Additional photograph's and information about Westfield's whip companies and the men that ran them can be found in the Westfield Athenaeum Archives under family files, whip company records and assorted other archived materials in addition to the various references listed in the bibliography.

Hopefully, this compilation has provided a perspective of how the whip industry was so important to Westfield, Massachusetts. Much remains to be considered by future researchers in developing more detailed company profiles or biographical sketches of the individual whip manufacturers.

If I have helped educate current generations with understanding the significance of Westfield's whip companies in both the whip industry and the town's development, while also assisting with future efforts on researching Westfield whip history, I will have accomplished my goal.

Bruce W. Cortis

Appendixes

John Thorpe Patent Application Letter, 1821

United States Patent   Patent No: X3361

John Thorp

Letters Patent

The schedule referred to in these Letters Patent and making part of the same containing a description in the words of the said John Thorp himself of his improvement being a Braiding Machine.

This machine consists of racers, the number of which is in proportion to the kind of braid or the number of strands that forms it. These wheels are placed in a circular frame, so that the carriers will have a direction pointing to the center where the braid is formed. The inner surface of said which are concave forming a curve corresponding with the circle on which they stand and are of an …. thickness connected one with another by cogs causing them to turn all together, and accurately on their circles, each forming its resolution in a proper line.

    There are two plates, whose surfaces form the same curve of the said wheels, one of which has a shaft confined to and extending from its center, passing loosely through the center of the other steadying it.

    These plates, which together constitute what I call a carrier and is that part of the machine, which contains and carries a spool, bobbin or a strand, and are as many in number as the threads or strands required to form the braid, each of which is placed astride upon the rims of said wheels and is pressed together by a spring which causes them to pinch the wheels producing a pincher sufficient to hold them in their places and is carried round in their proper route by the wheels as they turn shifting in their interoccurrence from one wheel to another, which is affected by <u>arms or Studs.</u>   These arms or studs are confined one to the carrier, and another Steadfastly fixed to some permanent part of the frame, with its point extending to near to where the rims of the wheels come in contact as to interfere with the point of the one belonging to the carrier, and their position are such as to crowd the said

United States Patent   Patent No: X3361

carriers from the rim of one wheel on to the rim of another and so on round, from wheel to wheel alternately forming the braid.

In the rims of said wheel are notches in which the shaft of the carriers lie and by which they are steadied in the circulation. These notches are so arranged as to occur exactly opposite each other, admitting the shaft of the carriers to press between the wheel as they turn. There are other small notches in said wheels which receive a projection from the carriers serving also to keep them in their place.

Said Machine is capable of making nearly all kinds of braid, such as whip thongs both single and twilled also the flat braids, single and twilled cords and will work from three strands to almost any number; and being constructed to operate without shuttles renders it subject to no sudden vibration, nor abruptness in its operation as the strands or threads that form the braid all circulate regularly without obstruction or impediment of motion.

To convert one of these machines which is calculated for braiding cord into one that will form a flat braid, no other alteration is necessary than to deprive it of a part of its wheels, letting the carrier return back and forth, instead of continuing round the wide circle.

It is necessary in making flat braid to have the outside or end wheels either smaller or larger so as not to lodge the carrier in the same place to which they were taken. The braid is taken forward by a weight or feeding rollers.

John Thorp

Witnesses
 William Atkin
 William Brian Staples

(Augt 10, 1821 *Patented*)

Westfield Whip Manufacturers – Sorted by Name

Westfield Whip Manufacturers – Sorted by name

Name	First	Last	Comment
Allen, Frank	1889	1890	
Allen, S. A. & Co.	1881	1890	
American Brass & Rivet	1892	1893	Buttons/Mountings
American Holly Whip	1894	1930	Holly Whips
American Whip Co.	1855	1933	
Ames, Etta C.	1886	1887	Snaps
Anderson, Samuel	1882	1888	
Arnold, Daniel B	1883	1883	Plaiting/Coverings
Arthur, Franklin	1850	1857	
Atlantic Whip Co.	1888	1923	
Atwater Geo. P. & Co.	1887	1896	
Atwater, Clark & Co.	1880	1881	
Atwater, Dwight M.	1874	1881	
Avery, A & D	1866	1873	Plaiting/Coverings
Avery, Dexter	1875	1881	Plaiting/Coverings
Avery, Horace W, Frank H & Horace	1872	1939	Lashes
Bailey, H. B.	1885	1886	
Bailey, W. G. & Co.	1875	1883	
Banner Whip	1909	1913	
Barnes & Kellogg	1872	1872	
Barnes Whip Co.	1888	1888	
Barnes, A. C. & Co. (1)	1884	1889	
Barnes, A. C. & Co. (2)	1889	1904	
Barnes, Beals & Co.	1872	1872	
Barnes, J.M.	1870	1897	Lashes
Barnes, Jay M.	1865	1874	
Barry Whip Co. (1)	1914	1921	
Barry Whip Co. (2)	1923	1938	

Westfield Whip Manufacturers – Sorted by name

Name	First	Last	Comment
Barstow & Co.	1882	1883	
Bay State Whip Co.	1887	1923	
Beals & Higgins	1880	1880	
Beals, L. H. & Co. (& Son after1885)	1867	1915	
Becker, Chas. G.	1893	1895	Stocks
Beebe, Henry C. & Co,	1867	1867	
Belden, D. L. & Co	1890	1891	Toy Whips
Berkshire Whip Co.	1896	1898	
Bishop, Lay & Co.	1873	1874	
Blodgett, George S.	1891	1894	Stocks
Bohler & Mackintosh	1880	1881	
Bohler & Phinney	1865		
Bohler, John J.	1865	1897	Stocks
Bohler, John J.	1873	1879	
Boynton & Brothers	1867	1867	
Bradley, Jesse M.	1880	1886	Lashes
Braman, L.D.	1885	1898	Lashes
Brass, W.	1867	1867	Plaiting/Coverings
Breckenbridge, Orlo	1873	1890	
Brooks, Peter	1872	1872	Plaiting/Coverings
Burke, T	1892	1892	
Bush, H J	1870	1870	
Bush, Henry	1894	1898	
Campbell, Andrew	1870	1874	Stocks
Campbell, Andrew	1872	1874	
Cargill, Cleveland & Co.	1905	1951	
Cargill, Cook & Co.	1884	1905	
Chadwick & Breckenbridge	1872	1872	
Chadwick, A. E.	1850	1850	
Chadwick, Samuel E	1878	1879	
Chapman & Barnes	1885	1885	

Westfield Whip Manufacturers – Sorted by name

Name	First	Last	Comment
Chapman & Grant	1885	1887	
Chapman & Thomas	1860	1860	
Chapman E. A.	1879	1879	Lashes
Chapman, C. C.	1880	1880	Lashes
Clark & Noyes Co.	1904	1930	
Clark, Atwater & Co.	1880	1880	
Clark, C. H.	1902	1906	
Clark, Oscar	1870	1882	
Coburn Whip	1872	1923	
Columbia Whip Co.	1892	1892	
Consolidated Whip Co.	1904	1923	
Continental Whip	1911	1923	
Cook & Parker	1888	1923	
Cook A.J. Whip Co.	1905	1912	
Cooley, Fuller & Cooper	1872	1872	
Cooper & Austin	1886	1886	
Cooper & Crouse	1886	1886	
Cooper, Edmund	1878	1892	
Cooper, Francis & Co.	1867	1867	
Cooper, Frank	1872	1872	
Couse, Fred P. & Son	1887	1915	
Cowles & Atwater	1872	1872	
Cowles & Horan	1913	1930	
Cowles & Sperry	1902	1902	
Crescent Whip Co	1907	1914	Toy & Riding
Dakin & Ferris	1897	1897	Machinery
Daniels, Wolcott	1889	1902	
Danks & Pease	1872	1872	
Danks & Son	1874	1878	
Danks, George L	1887	1888	
Darling, Smith & Co.	1854	1872	
Day, M. Jr & Co.	1850	1850	

Westfield Whip Manufacturers – Sorted by name

Name	First	Last	Comment
Dibble & Randall	1872	1886	Stocks
Dibble, Alfred	1887	1895	Stocks
Dickey, Louis	1872	1879	
Donovan Bros	1885	1893	Lashes
Donovan, C.F.	1885	1887	Lashes
Donovan, M.	1876	1876	
Dougherty Bros.	1887	1887	
Douglass T.	1865	1867	
Douglass, Chas & Co.	1873	1889	Toy & Riding
Dow & Gillett	1854	1854	
Dow, Loomis & Co	1852	1853	
Dow, Samuel & Co.	1836	1855	
Ely, Joseph Minor	1857	1885	
Empire Whip	1909	1914	
Ensign, Salmon	1878	1901	
Featherbone Whip Co.	1906	1922	
Fogg & Ladd	1894	1895	Machinery
Franklin Whip Co.	1897	1897	
Fuller & Cooper	1873	1876	
Fuller, A.D. (& Son)	1879	1896	Toy Whips
Fuller, A.D. Mrs.	1887	1897	Snaps
Fuller, Ellsworth S	1891	1898	
Fuller, J. B. & Co.	1876	1882	
Furrow, Richard	1852	1853	
Furrows, Albert W.	1872	1872	
Furrows, W. H.	1873	1873	
Gillett, Spencer & Co.	1860	1860	
Gillett & Weatherby	1865	1865	
Gillette, J.R.	1870	1870	
Gillett, L. C. & Co.	1860	1860	
Goff Derrick, N.	1872	1888	Lashes
Goff, Fred. E.	1886	1888	

Westfield Whip Manufacturers – Sorted by name

Name	First	Last	Comment
Grant, Frank G.	1850	1850	
Grant, Lemuel	1872	1889	Lashes
Great American Leather Co.	1962	1967	
Griffin, Duane D.	1874	1878	Plaiting/machinery
Griffin, J.E.	1885	1887	Stocks/Machinery
Gross, J. L. & Co.	1844	1857	
Gross, Jonah	1844	1857	
Hadley, Charles B.	1872	1893	Turner/Stocks
Hadley, Wilbur E.	1886	1892	
Hammersly, H. W.	1890	1892	
Hampden Whip Co.	1874	1883	
Harmonica Whip Co.	1877	1878	
Harrison, Hiram & Co.	1833	1855	
Hassler, C.W.	1905	1925	
Hastings, C.A.	1892	1911	Machinery
Hastings, Jonathan	1880	1888	Stocks
Henderson, Edward	1872	1872	
Henderson, Edward	1872	1872	Machinery
High Speed Braider Co.	1891	1893	Machinery
Holcomb & Cook	1875	1887	
Holcomb & Loomis	1850	1850	
Holcomb & Weatherby	1860	1860	
Holcomb, Eustace, H.	1872	1872	
Holcomb, Hial	1834	1860	
Holcomb, Lester	1860	1860	
Holly Whip Co.	1902	1902	
Holmes, David	1872	1872	
Horse Whip Co.	1901	1933	
Hosmer. W. W.	1885	1909	
Hubbard, Ezra	1850	1850	
Hull, Hiram	1822	1855	
Independent Whip	1894	1930	

Westfield Whip Manufacturers – Sorted by name

Name	First	Last	Comment
International Whip	1911	1917	
Jones Emerson S.	1872	1883	Thongs/Lashes
Judson, L. O.	1873	1873	
King Whip Joseph, Jos & Son)	1865	1898	
King, Gamaliel	1860	1895	
Knowles & Hastings	1872	1879	
Knowles & Kellogg	1867	1867	
Knowles M.D. & Co.	1876	1876	
Knowles, Josiah S.	1850	1872	
Laflin, James	1876	1876	Mountings
Lamberton, D.	1870	1870	
Lambson, William L.	1860	1870	
Lay & Webb	1882	1882	
Lay Whip Co.	1887	1923	
Lay, Barber & Co.	1883	1884	
Lay, Barber & Lay	1881	1883	
Lay, Edwin R.	1873	1878	
Lay, Edwin R. & Son	1878	1880	
Lay, Van Deusen & Co.	1885	1885	
Lemon, Gideon	1886	1887	
Lewis, L. B.	1872	1888	
Lewis, L. M.	1850	1850	
Lewis, Lyman H.	1850	1850	
Lewis, Merrick	1852	1852	
Light, Edward B., Light Whip Company	1870	1874	
Lombard, H.	1876	1876	
Loomis & Becker	1885	1886	Buttons/Mounts
Loomis & Nelson	1850	1850	
Loomis, Atwater & Co.	1852	1867	
Loomis, Don & Co.	1850	1850	
Loomis, Frank (F.D. & Son)	1888	1898	Buttons

Westfield Whip Manufacturers – Sorted by name

Name	First	Last	Comment
Loomis, John	1850	1850	
Loomis, Lester	1860	1878	Lashes
Loomis, Lester (Leicester)	1855	1878	Thongs/Lashes
Loomis, R	1850	1850	
Loomis, Silas	1887	1891	Stocks
Lounsbury, J.H.	1891	1907	Machinery
Mackintosh, Royal A.	1883	1883	Snaps
Mallory, C. B.	1853	1853	
Massasoit Whip	1889	1923	
Mercantile Whip Co.	1903	1903	
Mesick & Atwater	1886	1886	
Mesick Bros.	1896	1896	
Mesick, George	1897	1898	
Mesick, Jas. E	1881	1898	
Miller, Emerson S.	1874	1878	
Miller, James	1850	1874	
Moore, George	1874	1889	Plaiting/Coverings
Moore, M.E. (& Son)	1883	1914	Machinery
Mullen, Henry J	1893	1898	Buttons
Mundale Whip Co.	1872	1876	
Munroe, Brownson & Co.	1850	1853	
National Knot Co	1905	1905	
National Manufacturing Co.	1894	1898	
National Whip Co. (I)	1873	1876	
National Whip Co. (II)	1911	1928	
New England Whip Co.	1890	1926	
Noble, James	1834	1853	
Obrien & Krollman	1875	1875	
Osborn, John	1887	1887	
Osden Whip Co.	1881	1883	
Osden, Frank M.	1886	1897	
Osden, L. M. & Brother	1867	1874	

Westfield Whip Manufacturers – Sorted by name

Name	First	Last	Comment
Owen, Osden & Co.	1874	1878	
Owen, William H.	1878	1893	
Palmer & Upson	1896	1915	Buttons
Palmer, H. A.	1894	1895	Machinery
Pease, Frederick	1860	1867	Lashes
Peck & Whipple Co	1884	1926	
Peck, George S. & Co. (1)	1872	1877	
Peck, George S. & Co. (2)	1881	1884	
Peck, Osden & Co.	1878	1881	
Pendleton & Braman	1883	1883	Lashes
Phelps, Eben & Co.	1860	1867	
Phelps, Edwin	1850	1886	
Phelps, Enoch	1879	1898	Lashes
Philadelphia Whip Snap Co.	1894	1894	Snaps
Pomeroy & Van Deusen	1886	1902	
Pratt, Atwater & Co.	1870	1872	
Pratt, Atwater & Goodnow	1872	1872	
Pratt, Atwater & Owen	1872	1874	
Pratt, C. C.	1865		
Provin, Wm.	1849	1902	
Rand, J.R., & Son, Rand & Co.	1833	1870	
Rand, Lewis & Rand	1867	1867	
Reed, Thomas	1886	1887	
Reliance Whip	1908	1913	
Richardson	1873		
Rising, A. A.	1882	1883	Stocks
Rogers Bros	1876	1879	
Root, O	1876	1876	
Sackett, Dudley	1850	1850	
Sackett, George	1860	1878	Lashes
Sackett, Herman	1865	1867	

Westfield Whip Manufacturers – Sorted by name

Name	First	Last	Comment
Sanford Whip Co.	1880	1923	
Scheip Robt & Co.	1905	1910	Toy & Riding
Schmidt, E. F.	1886	1912	
Schmidt, John C. & Co.	1867	1901	
Scott Bros	1887	1887	
Searle Whip, Frank P. Searle (1)	1889	1905	
Searle, Frank P. (2)	1882	1892	
Shepard, Holcomb & Cook	1860	1875	
Shepard, J. L. & Brothers	1860	1867	
Shepard, Solomon	1837	1850	
Sherman, Wm. T.	1893	1895	Stocks
Sizer, Ephraim	1852	1852	
Sizer, Emerson	1856	1879	Machinery
Smith & Perry	1872	1872	
Smith J. T. & Son	1874	1874	
Smith James T.	1867	1867	
Smith Lockwood Co	1910	1920	
Smith R. J. & Son	1870	1876	
Smith, Andrew, J.	1874	1879	
Smith, Henry	1875	1875	
Specialty Whip Co	1913	1920	
Spencer, Chas W.	1846	1892	
Spencer-Martin Whip Co.	1906	1916	
Sperry, A.	1850	1850	
Standard Whip Co.	1881	1924	
Steimer & Moore Mfg. Co.	1889	1918	
Steimer & Searle & Co.	1883	1889	
Steimer, Leonard W.	1879	1882	
Sterling Whip Co.	1904	1915	
Stevens, Wolcott	1879	1885	
Stiles, Henry b.	1891	1898	Lashes
Stringfellow, Edwin	1897	1897	

Westfield Whip Manufacturers – Sorted by name

Name	First	Last	Comment
Swan, Adam	1879	1879	
Swan, Edward	1860	1867	
Sweatland & Lawler	1890	1890	Holly Whips
Sweatland, L.R. & Co.	1891	1910	Holly Whips
Talmadge, Wm. H.	1890	1898	Toy Whips
Textile Mfg. Co.	1886		Buttons
Thomas, A. H.	1882	1883	Lashes
Tyler Whip	1911	1930	
Tyler, N.F.	1879	1891	Coverings machinery
U.S. Whip Co.	1892	1935	
Union Whip Co.	1883	1886	
Van Deusen Brothers (I)	1860	1868	
Van Deusen Brothers (II)	1876	1878	
Van Deusen, H.M. Whip Co.	1902	1930	
Velten, Ludwig	1886	1893	Mountings
Webb, Henry	1885	1890	Lashes
Westfield Platting Co.	1882	1897	Plaiting/Coverings
Westfield Whip Co. (I)	1870	1873	
Westfield Whip Co. (II)	1884	1930	
Westfield Whip Mfg. Co.	1946	2018	
Westfield Whip Snap Works	1894	1902	Snaps
Westfield Whip Socket Co.	1879	1879	Mountings
Whipple Charles M. & Co.	1872	1884	
Whipple, George E.	1885	1897	Mountings
Whipple, James P. (& Son)	1867	1883	Mountings
Williams & Van Deusen Mfg.	1890	1890	Buttons
Woodbury Whip	1865	1930	
Woronoco Whip Co	1903	1903	
Wright, Lucius	1885	1887	Stocks

Westfield Whip Patents Sorted by Year and Number

Including the patents of Liverus Hull while running the Whip convict shop at Charlestown, Ma for American Whip and other towns connected to Westfield

Unless otherwise noted, patents are from Westfield.

Westfield Whip Patents Sorted by Year and Number

Year	Number	Name(s)	Description	Location
1832	x7.017	Dayton, Giles & Mallory, Andrew	Lathe for Turning Whip Stocks	Blandford Russell
1832	n/a	Morgan, Frederick	Varnish for applying to Whip Stocks	
1836	43	Alvord, Enos & Nelson	Lathe for Turning & c.	
1838	672	Halladay, Seymour	Plaiting Machine for Covering Whip	
1840	1476	Sackett, Dudley D	Improvements to Halladay Braiding Machines	
1850	7,068	Day, D.N. & E.B.	Whip Lash	
1854	10,718	Sizer, Ephraim & Titus	Improvement to Sacket's Braiding Machine	
1855	13,354	Hull, Liverus	Machine for Sawing Rattan	Charlestown
	13,391	Hull, Liverus	Braiding Machines	Charlestown
	13,719	Hull, Liverus	Improved Braiding Machinery	Charlestown
1856	14,612	Hull, Liverus	Machine for Tapering Whalebone	Charlestown
1866	52,718	Hull, Liverus	Machine for Weaving Whip Coverings	Charlestown

Westfield Whip Patents Sorted by Year and Number

Year	Number	Name(s)	Description	Location
1866	53,003	Hull, Liverus	Turning Lathe for Wood	Charlestown
1866	56,419	Hull, Liverus	Lathe for Turning Whip Stocks	Charlestown
1867	61,070	Hull, Liverus	Improved Whip Stock	Charlestown
	65,917	King, Gamaliel & Pratt, Charles	Improved Method of covering whips - waterproofing of stock	
	70,501	Axtell, Henry	Whip Rolling Machine	Huntington
1868	77,477	Gillett	Improvement of Whips, moisture proofing	
	78,129	Rand, Addison C.	Improved Process for Covering Whips	
	79,299	Avery, Dexter	Improvement of whips, interwoven threads instead of braiding	
	81,507	Hull, Liverus	Improvement of whips using India Rubber vulcanizing	Charleston
	82,840	Hull, Liverus	Improved Whip Handle	Charleston
	RE2925	King, Gamaliel & Pratt, Charles C.	Improvement in covering whips	
	RE2926	King, Gamaliel & Pratt, Charles C.	Improvement in covering whips	
1869	87,268	Knowles, M.D.	Improved Covering for Whips	
	87,836	Gillett, James R	Whip Mounting	

Westfield Whip Patents Sorted by Year and Number

Year	Number	Name(s)	Description	Location
	89,168	Rand, Addison C.	Improved Whip Braiding	
	89,487	King, Gamaliel	Improvement in loading of whips	
	RE3754	Hull, Liverus	Improved Whip Stock reissue of 610070	Charlestown
1870	102,007	Hull, Liverus	Use of Metal wire in Stock	Charleston
	101,912	Rand, Addison C	Wire Whalebone Replacement	
	101,913	Rand, Addison C	Two piece stock, different cores	
	101,914	Rand, Addison C	Spiral outer wrapping	
	101,915	Rand, Addison C	Improvement, Metal Core in stock	
	102,863	Rand, Addison C	Use of wire wound in a spiral form in stock	
	103,467	Hull, Liverus	Ratan Glued to Central core of Whalebone	Charleston
	104,433	Crowsen, Velenus W.	Waterproof cover of raw gutta-percha to whipstocks	
1871	112,891	Bohler, John J.	Whip completely made of leather	
	119,296	Avery, Horace W	Improvement of Whip stocks construction	
	120,782	Sizer, Emerson	Whip Braiding machine	
	121,761	Crowson, Velenus W.	Covering for Whips	

Westfield Whip Patents Sorted by Year and Number

Year	Number	Name(s)	Description	Location
1872	124,070	Light, Edward B.	Whip Lash	
	125,134	Holmes, David	Covering for Whip Stocks	
	126,631	Goff, Derrick N.	Covering for Whip Handles	
	131,975	Schmidt, John C.	Whip Lash	
	132,909	Hull, David C.	Construction Whip Stocks	
	133,946	Light, Edward B.	Whip Lash & Snap	
1873	137,341	Bush, Henry J.	Whip Lash	
	143,065	Couse, Frederic P	Improvement to Whips	
	RE5651	Hull, David C.	Improvement to 132,909	
	RE5651	Hull, David C.	Whip Stocks	
1874	149,571	Bush, Henry J.	Whip Stock Covering	
	153,041	Bohler, John J.	Whip forming molds	
	153,517	Avery, Dexter & Pratt, Charles C.	Construction	
	153,762	Douglas	Rubber Covering for Whip Stock	
	154,211	Avery, Dexter & Pratt, Charles C.	Taper Whip Stocks	
	155,412	Bohler, John J	Covering	
	Res960	Holmes, David	Artificial Veneers	
1875	162,605	Bohler, John J	Socket Joint for Whip Canes	
	175,639	Avery, Dexter	Whip Ferrule	
	176,958	Hull, David C	Improved Button & Ferrule	
	180,026	Hartwell, Charles	Chuck for turning whip stocks	

Westfield Whip Patents Sorted by Year and Number

Year	Number	Name(s)	Description	Location
	182,790	Avery, Dexter	Loading of Stock	
	183,449	Daniels, Wolcott O.	Button	
	RE7262	Hull, Liverus	Reissue of 53,003 assign to Amer Whip	Charleston
1877	189,569	Moore, Moses E	Improvement in Machine for Whip Sides	
	192,617	Beckenridge, Orlo	Connection	
	196,827	Rice, Walter H	Whip & Cane Handle Improvements	
1878	318,348	Bryant, Orin & Ring, Elkinah	Whip Stock machine	
	208,249	Lombard, Hezekial	Whip Rounding Machine	
1879	212,891	Bryant, Orrin	Whip Rolling Machine	
	214,257	Lombard, Hezekial	Whip Rounding Machine	
1880	227,391	Schmidt, John C.	Whip Handle	
	227,392	Schmidt, John C.	Whip Handle	
	232,179	Gilman, Myron A	Cane & Whip Handle	
	232,452	Bush, Henry J.	Ferrule	
	232,670	Bohler, John J & Phinney, Ezra S.	Whip Snap	
	233,613	Gilman, Myron A.	Toy Whip & Cane	
	234,769	Gilman, Myron A.	Whip Handles	
1881	236,357	Pratt, Charles C.	Whip Wrap	
	240,381	Bush, Henry J.	Rattan Whip Gut Core	
	240,750	Mullen, Henry	Whip Lash Coupling	

223

Westfield Whip Patents Sorted by Year and Number

Year	Number	Name(s)	Description	Location
	242,749	Campbell, Andrew Jr.	Whip Handle	
	244,619	King, Gamaliel	Replacement to Whalebone	
	246,041	Shepard, Charles F.	Whip Core and Whip	
	249,855	Mullen, Henry	Whip Core and Whip	
	250,162	Mullen, Henry & Noble, James Jr.	Improvement to Braiding	
1882	255,131	Barstow, Vinal B. & Mallory, Stanton H.	New Whip Core	
	256,031	Mullen, Henry & Noble, James Jr.	New Whip Core	
	259,320	Lakin, James A	Loop Fastening	
	261,550	Hull, David C.	Use of Spike to increase size of Ratan	
	263,098	Barstow, Vinal B.	Inexpensive Whip	
1883	274,641	Mullen, Henry & Noble, James Jr.	Loop Fastening	
	277,778	Phelps, Enoch	Whip Coupling	
	277,967	Williams, Charles	Machine for Twisting Snaps	
	281,305	Schmidt, John C.	Manufacture of Whip	
	288,305	Bush, Henry J.	Celluloid Covering	
1884	293,954	Daniels, Wolcott O.	Whip mount for Button	
	297,006	Rand, Alonzo C.	Tightening Screw	
1885	315,653	Mullen, Henry & Noble, James Jr.	Whip Core	

Westfield Whip Patents Sorted by Year and Number

Year	Number	Name(s)	Description	Location
	318,432	Mullen, Henry & Noble, James Jr.	Whip Stock	
	327,746	Wilson, Spear & Pierce	Whip Core	
1886	341,795	Couse, Frederick P	Lash Loop	
	343,721	Becker, Charles G. & Morgan, Hubert W.	Button	
	344,979	Mullen, Henry & Noble, James Jr.	Whip Core	
	345,166	Morse, William J.	Whip Button	
	351,522	Parker, Erastus N.	Lash Loop	Springfield
	353,371	Mullen, Henry	Snapper Loops	
1887	356,092	Becker, Charles G.	Whip Button	
	360,718	Moore, George T.	Whip Snap	
	361,034	Williams, Charles E.	Whip Button	
	361,035	Williams, Charles E.	Disk Whip Head	
	367,761	Mullen, Henry & Noble, James Jr.	Whip Rolling Machine	
	373,165	Williams, Charles E	Cap	
	373,166	Williams, Charles E.	Button	
	373,167	Williams, Charles E.	Button	
	375,473	Bradley, Charles J.	Machine for Laying Buttton Molds on Whips	
1888	375,984	Bohler, John J.	Whip Lash	
1889	397,456	Cowles, Henry A.	Whip	
	407,690	Ring, Elkinah	Whip Rolling Machine	

Westfield Whip Patents Sorted by Year and Number

Year	Number	Name(s)	Description	Location
	407,691	Ring, Elkinah	Whip Rolling Machine	
	417,172	Griffin, Duane D.	Braiding Machine	
	417,203	Ring, Elkinah	Whip Center	
1890	426,419	Sullivan, John T.	Whip	
	423,725	Bradley, Charles J.	Whip	
	432,486	Gowdy, Rvillo T.	Whip	
	439,943	Griffin, Duane D.	Feed Attachment for Braiding Machines	
1891	444,250	Mullen, Henry	Inexpensive Whip	
	448,650	Grant, Frank	Waterproof Whip	
	451,028	Cowles, Ezra A.	Whip	
	452,327	Noble, James Jr. & Whipple, George E.	Whip Lining	
1892	469,897	Grant, Frank & Veltin, Ludwig	Ferrules, Method for making	
	472,869	Foley, Frank	Whip Core	
	473,695	Couse, Frederich P.	Rawhide Center, Waterproof, Inexpensive	
	D21817	Pomeroy, Julian	Design for a Whip	Springfield
1893	491,512	Becker, Charles G.	Cap	
	492,606	Bush, Henry J.	Rattan Center	
	500,096	Daniels, Wolcott O.	Whip	
	503,332	Sanford, Frederick A.	Whip	
	508,937	Griffin, Duane D.	Stalk Splitting Machine for Rattan	

Westfield Whip Patents Sorted by Year and Number

Year	Number	Name(s)	Description	Location
1894	511,816	Moore, George T. & Steimer, Leonard W.	Whip stock core	
1898	597,614	Levie, Charles A	Machine for Unwinding Ropes from Whip Stocks	
	600,171	Pratt, Charles C.	Cap/Button	
	608,315	Becker, Charles G & Osborn, Martin	Process for Treating Rawhide	
1899	633,433	Donovan, John P.	Mach for Twisting and Stretching Rawhide	
	629,886	Beman, Herbert D.	Whip	
	630,665	Couse, Frederich P	Loading of Whip Butts	
	631,548	Van Deusen, Henry M.	Whip Load	
	D31468	Van Deusen, Henry M.	Design for Whip Load	
1900	634,009	Hull, David C.	Butt Load	
	643,294	Hull, David C.	Whip Stock	
	D32438	Van Deusen, Henry M.	Whip Load	
	649,675	Pomeroy, Julian	Method of making whip	Springfield
	649,677	Larson, Henry W & Pomeroy, Julian	Strip of Matter	Springfield
	649,679	Larson, Henry W & Pomeroy, Julian	Strip of Matter	Springfield
	D32742	Van Deusen, Henry M	Design for Whip Load	

227

Westfield Whip Patents Sorted by Year and Number

Year	Number	Name(s)	Description	Location
1901	D34009	Hull, David C.	Whip Load	
	D34200	Hull, David C.	Butt Load	
	683,276	Hassler, Charles W.	Whip Braider Tensioner	
1902	707,124	Larsson, Henry W.	Butt Loading for Whips	
	711,897	Hull, David C.	Whip	
1903	732,917	Beals, Luther L.	Whip	
	737,352	Cook, Arthur J.	Whip Load	
1904	749,290	Hassler, Charles W.	Racer for braiding Machines	
	769,516	Van Deusen, Henry M.	Drop Top Whip	
	770,813	Larrson, Henry W.	Whip Making Machine	Springfield
	776,842	Horwood, Thomas	Braided Cord	
1905	783400	Cowles, Frank E	Whip	
1906	832,272	Palmer, Henry A.	Whip Button Methods	
1907	846,458	Donovan, John P.	String Tapering Machine for Whip	
	861,653	Hull, David C.	Crimper & Tucker for Whip Buttons	
1909	919202	Moore, Clarence M.	Rattan Straitening machine	Mitteneague
1910	977,670	Beman, Herbet D. & McLaughlln, John	Whip Button	
1911	981,147	Whipple, George E.	Whip Core	
	983,057	Hull, David C.	Whip	
1916	1,181,950	Donovan, Cornelius & Donovan, John P.	Improvement to Whip Centers	

Westfield Whip Patents Sorted by Year and Number

Year	Number	Name(s)	Description	Location
1917	1,250,561	Clark, Charles H.	Whip construction improvement	

Westfield Whip Patents Sorted by Name

Including the patents of Liverus Hull while running the Whip convict shop at Charlestown, Ma for American Whip and other towns connected to Westfield

Unless otherwise noted, patents are from Westfield.

Westfield Whip Patents Sorted by Name

Last Name	First Name	Number	Year	Description
Alvord	Enos & Nelson	43	1836	Lathe for Turning & c.
Avery	Dexter	79,299	1868	Improvement of whips, interwoven threads instead of braiding
Avery	Horace W	119,296	1871	Improvement of Whip stocks construction
Avery	Dexter	153,517	1874	Construction
Avery	Dexter	154,211	1874	Taper Whip Stocks
Avery	Dexter	175,639	1876	Whip Ferrule
Avery	Dexter	182,790	1876	Loading of Stock
Barstow	Vinal B	255,131	1882	New Whip Core
Barstow	Vinal B	263,098	1882	Inexpensive Whip
Barstow	Vinal B	263,098	1882	Inexpensive Whip
Beals	Luther H	732,917	1903	Whip
Breckenbridge	Orlo	192,617	1877	Connection
Becker	Charles G	343,721	1886	Button
Becker	Charles G	356,092	1887	Whip Button
Becker	Charles G	491,512	1893	Cap
Becker	Charles G	608,315	1898	Process for Treating Rawhide
Beman	Herbert D	629,886	1899	Whip
Beman	Herbert D	977,670	1910	Whip Button

Westfield Whip Patents Sorted by Name

Last Name	First Name	Number	Year	Description
Bohler	John J	112,891	1871	Whip completely made of leather
Bohler	John J	153,041	1874	Whip forming molds
Bohler	John J	155,412	1874	Covering
Bohler	John J	162,605	1875	Socket Joint for Whip Canes
Bohler	John J	232,670	1880	Whip Snap
Bohler	John J	375,984	1888	Whip Lash
Bradley	Charles J	375,473	1887	Machine for Laying Buttton Molds on Whips
Bradley	Charles J	423,725	1890	Whip
Bryant	Orrin	212,891	1879	Whip Rolling Machine
Bryant	Orrin	318,348	1878	Whip Stock machine
Bush	Henry J	137,341	1873	Whip Lash
Bush	Henry J	149,571	1874	Whip Stock Covering
Bush	Henry J	232,452	1880	Ferrule
Bush	Henry J	240,381	1881	Rattan Whip Gut Core
Bush	Henry J	288,305	1883	Celluloid Covering
Bush	Henry J	492,606	1893	Rattan Center
Campbell	Andrew, 2nd	242,749	1881	Whip Handle
Clark	Charles H	1,250,561	1917	Whip construction improvement
Comstock	Charles M	226,495	1880	Machine for Rolling Whips
Comstock	Charles M	354,395	1886	Whip Snap
Comstock	Charles M	393,691	1888	Whip Core
Cook	Arthur J	737,352	1903	Whip Load

Westfield Whip Patents Sorted by Name

Last Name	First Name	Number	Year	Description
Cooper	Francis	245,706	1881	Whip Coupling
Couse	Frederic P	143,065	1873	Improvement to Whips
Couse	Frederick P	341,795	1886	Lash Loop
Couse	Frederich P	473,695	1892	Rawhide Center, Waterproof, Inexpensive
Couse	Frederich P	630,665	1899	Loading of Whip Butts
Cowles	Henry A	397,456	1889	Whip
Cowles	Ezra A	451,028	1891	Whip
Cowles	Frank E	783400	1905	Whip
Crowsen	Velenus W	104,433	1870	Waterproof cover of raw gutta-percha to whipstocks
Crowson	Velenus W	121,761	1871	Covering for Whips
Cushman	Henry S	378,662	1888	Whip Stock Core
Cushman	Henry S	472,919	1892	Cheap Durable Whip Core
Daniels	Wolcott O	183,449	1876	Button
Daniels	Wolcott O	293,954	1884	Whip mount for Button
Daniels	Wolcott O	500,096	1893	Whip
Day	D N	7,068	1850	Whip Lash
Day	E B	7,068	1850	Whip Lash
Donovan	John P	633,433	1899	Mach for Twisting and Strething Rawhide
Donovan	John P	846,458	1907	String Tapering Machine for Whip
Donovan	Cornelius F	1,181,950	1916	Improvement to Whip Centers
Donovan	John P	1,181,950	1916	Improvement to Whip Centers

Westfield Whip Patents Sorted by Name

Last Name	First Name	Number	Year	Description
Douglas	George C	153,762	1874	Rubber Covering for Whip Stock
Foley	Frank	472,869	1892	Whip Core
Gillett	James R	77,477	1868	Improvement of Whips, moisture proofing
Gillett	James R	87,836	1869	Whip Mounting
Gilman	Myron A	232,179	1880	Cane & Whip Handle
Gilman	Myron A	233,613	1880	Toy Whip & Cane
Gilman	Myron A	234,769	1880	Whip Handles
Goff	Derick N	126,631	1872	Covering for Whip Handles
Goodenough	Franklin L	374,532	1887	Machine for setting caps on whips
Gowdy	Revilo T	432,486	1890	Whip
Grant	Frank	448,650	1891	Waterproof Whip
Grant	Frank	469,897	1892	Ferrules, Method for making
Griffin	Duane D.	417,172	1889	Braiding Machine
Griffin	Duane D.	439,943	1890	Feed Attachment for Braiding Machines
Griffin	Duane D.	508,937	1893	Stalk Splitting Machine for Rattan
Halladay	Seymour	672	1838	Plaiting Machine for Covering Whip
Hartwell	Charles	180,026	1876	Chuck for turning whip stocks
Hassler	Charles W	683,276	1901	Whip Braider Tensioner
Hassler	Charles W	749,290	1904	Racer for braiding Machines
Holmes	David	125,134	1872	Covering for Whip Stocks

Westfield Whip Patents Sorted by Name

Last Name	First Name	Number	Year	Description
Holmes	David	Res960	1874	Artificial Veneers
Horwood	Thomas	776,842	1904	Braided Cord
Hull	Liverus	81,507	1868	Improvement of whips using India Rubber vulcanizing
Hull	Liverus	103,467	1870	Ratan Glued to Central core of Whalebone
Hull	Liverus	13,354	1855	Machine for Sawing Rattan
Hull	Liverus	13,391	1855	Braiding Machines
Hull	Liverus	13,719	1855	Improved Braiding Machinery
Hull	Liverus	14,612	1856	Machine for Tapering Whalebone
Hull	Liverus	52,718	1866	Machine for Weaving Whip Coverings
Hull	Liverus	53,003	1866	Turning Lathe for Wood
Hull	Liverus	54,167	1866	Elastic Webbing - Braid
Hull	Liverus	56,419	1866	Lathe for Turning Whip Stocks
Hull	Liverus	58,830	1866	Braiding Method
Hull	Liverus	61,070	1867	Improved Whip Stock
Hull	Liverus	82,840	1868	Improved Whip Handle
Hull	Liverus	RE3754	1869	Improved Whip Stock reissue of 610070
Hull	Liverus	102,007	1870	Use of Metal wire in Stock

Westfield Whip Patents Sorted by Name

Last Name	First Name	Number	Year	Description
Hull	David C	132,909	1872	Construction Whip Stocks
Hull	David C	RE5651	1873	Improvement to 132,909
Hull	David C	RE5651	1873	Whip Stocks
Hull	David C	176,958	1876	Improved Button & Ferrule
Hull	Liverus	RE7262	1876	Reissue of 53,003 assign to Amer Whip
Hull	David C	261,550	1882	Use of Spike to increase size of Ratan
Hull	David C	634,009	1900	Butt Load
Hull	David C	643,294	1900	Whip Stock
Hull	David C	D34009	1901	Whip Load
Hull	David C	D34200	1901	Butt Load
Hull	David C	711,897	1902	Whip
Hull	David C	861,653	1907	Crimper & Tucker for Whip Buttons
Hull	David C	983,057	1911	Whip
King	Gamaliel	65,917	1867	Improved Method of covering whips - waterproofing of stock
King	Gamaliel	RE2925	1868	Improvement in covering whips
King	Gamaliel	RE2926	1868	Improvement in covering whips
King	Gamaliel	89,487	1869	Improvement in loading of whips
King	Gamaliel	244,619	1881	Replacement to Whalebone
Knowles	M D	87,268	1869	Improved Covering for Whips

Westfield Whip Patents Sorted by Name

Last Name	First Name	Number	Year	Description
Lakin	James A	259,320	1882	Loop Fastening
Levie	Charles A	597,614	1898	Machine for Unwinding Ropes from Whip Stocks
Light	Edward B	124,070	1872	Whip Lash
Light	Edward B	133,946	1872	Whip Lash & Snap
Light	Edward B.	154,876	1874	Whip Tip Ferrule
Lombard	Hezekial	208,249	1878	Whip Rounding Machine
Lombard	Hezekiah	214,257	1879	Whip Rounding Machine
Mallory	Stanton H.	255,131	1882	New Whip Core
McLaughlin	John	977,670	1910	Whip Button
Moore	Moses E	189,569	1877	Improvement in Mach. for Whip Sides
Moore	George T	360,718	1887	Whip Snap
Moore	George T	511,816	1894	Whip stock core
Morgan	Fred	1	1832	Varnish for applying to Whip Stocks
Morgan	Hubert W	343,721	1886	Button
Morse	William J	345,166	1886	Whip Button
Mullen	Henry	240,750	1881	Whip Lash Coupling
Mullen	Henry	249,855	1881	Whip Core and Whip
Mullen	Henry	250,162	1881	Improvement to Braiding
Mullen	Henry	256,031	1882	New Whip Core
Mullen	Henry	274,641	1883	Loop Fastening
Mullen	Henry	315,653	1885	Whip Core
Mullen	Henry	318,432	1885	Whip Stock

Westfield Whip Patents Sorted by Name

Last Name	First Name	Number	Year	Description
Mullen	Henry	344,979	1886	Whip Core
Mullen	Henry	353,371	1886	Snapper Loops
Mullen	Henry	367,761	1887	Whip Rolling Machine
Mullen	Henry	444,250	1891	Inexpensive Whip
Noble	James, Jr.	250,162	1881	Improvement to Braiding
Noble	James, Jr.	256,031	1882	New Whip Core
Noble	James Jr.	274,641	1883	Loop Fastening
Noble	James Jr	315,653	1885	Whip Core
Noble	James Jr	318,432	1885	Whip Stock
Noble	James, Jr.	344,979	1886	Whip Core
Noble	James, Jr	367,761	1887	Whip Rolling Machine
Noble	James, Jr.	452,327	1891	Whip Lining
Osborn	Martin	608,315	1898	Process for Treating Rawhide
Palmer	Henry A	832,272	1906	Whip Button Methods
Phelps	Enoch	277,778	1883	Whip Coupling
Phinney	Ezra S	232,670	1880	Whip Snap
Pratt	Charles C	65,917	1867	Improved Method of covering whips - waterproofing of stock
Pratt	Charles C	RE2925	1868	Improvement in covering whips
Pratt	Charles C	RE2926	1868	Improvement in covering whips
Pratt	Charles C	153,517	1874	Construction
Pratt	Charles C	154,211	1874	Taper Whip Stocks
Pratt	Charles C	236,357	1881	Whip Wrap
Pratt	Charles C	600,171	1898	Cap/Button

Westfield Whip Patents Sorted by Name

Last Name	First Name	Number	Year	Description
Rand	Addison C	78,129	1868	Improved Process for Covering Whips
Rand	Addison C	89,168	1869	Improved Whip Braiding
Rand	Addison C	101,912	1870	Wire Whalebone Replacement
Rand	Addison C	101,913	1870	two piece stock different cores
Rand	Addison C	101,914	1870	Spiral outer wrapping
Rand	Addison C	101,915	1870	Improvement, Metal Core in stock
Rand	Addison C	102,863	1870	Use of wire wound in a spiral form in stock
Rand	Alonzo C	297,006	1884	Tightening Screw
Rice	Walter H	196,827	1877	Whip & Cane Handle Improvements
Ring	Elkinah	318,348	1878	Whip Stock machine
Ring	Elkanah	407,690	1889	Whip Rolling Machine
Ring	Elkanah	407,691	1889	Whip Rolling Machine
Ring	Elkanah	417,203	1889	Whip Center
Sackett	Dudley D	1476	1840	Improvements to Halladay Braiding Machines
Sanford	Frederick A.	503,332	1893	Whip
Schmidt	John C	131,975	1872	Whip Lash
Schmidt	John C	227,391	1880	Whip Handle
Schmidt	John C	227,392	1880	Whip Handle

Westfield Whip Patents Sorted by Name

Last Name	First Name	Number	Year	Description
Schmidt	John C.	281,305	1883	Manufacture of Whip
Shepard	Charles F	246,041	1881	Whip Core and Whip
Sizer	Ephraim	10,718	1854	Improvement to Sacket's Braiding Machine
Sizer	Titus	10,718	1854	Improvement to Sacket's Braiding Machine
Sizer	Emerson	120,782	1871	Whip Braiding machine
Steimer	Leonard W	511,816	1894	Whip stock core
Sullivan	John T	426,419	1890	Whip
Underwood	Wells A	460,456	1891	Whip Core
Van Deusen	Henry M	631,548	1899	Whip Load
Van Deusen	Henry M	D31468	1899	Design for Whip Load
Van Deusen	Henry M	D32438	1900	Whip Load
Van Deusen	Henry M	D32742	1900	Design for Whip Load
Van Deusen	Henry M	769,516	1904	Drop Top Whip
Veltin	Ludwig	469,897	1892	Ferrules, Method for making
Whipple	George E	452,327	1891	Whip Lining
Whipple	George E	981,147	1911	Whip Core
Williams	Charles	277,967	1883	Machine for Twisting Snaps
Williams	Charles E	361,034	1887	Whip Button
Williams	Charles E	361,035	1887	Disk Whip Head
Williams	Charles E	373,165	1887	Cap
Williams	Charles E	373,166	1887	Button
Williams	Charles E	373,167	1887	Button

Bibliography

Newspapers & Local Publications

Springfield, Union Newspaper, Springfield, Ma., multiple articles, dates as noted.

Springfield Republican Newspaper, Springfield, Ma. multiple articles, dates as noted

Valley Echo Newspaper, Westfield, Ma. Multiple articles, dates as noted

Westfield Times Newsletter, Westfield Mass. Multiple articles dates as noted.

Town of Westfield, Mass, Souvenir 1906, published by W.M. Alcorn Souvenir Association, Westfield Times Co. Print, Westfield

Multiple other newspaper accounts sourced from website GenealogyBank.com

Multiple personal accounts and local histories as noted in the text.

Massachusetts and Industry Publications

Westfield City Directories - 1872 – 1920

The Massachusetts Directory; being the first Part of the New England Directory, 1835 by John Hayward, pub: John Hayward, corner of Court and Tremont Street, Boston

Massachusetts State Directory, containing the names residences and business of every individual firm or company, engaged in any occupation in the State ... arranged for the year 1850-51, pub: S.B. Brooks & Geo. B. Haskell, Boston, Mass., 1851.

The Massachusetts Register for the year 1852 containing a Business Directory, pub: George Adams, 91 Washington Street, Boston, Mass.
(also same volume for year 1853)

Statistical Information relating to certain Branches of Industry in Massachusetts, for the year ending June 1, 1855, by Francis DeWitt, Secretary of the Commonwealth, William White, Printer to the State, 1856

The Massachusetts Register 1867 containing a record of State and County Offices and a Directory of Merchants, Manufacturers. Etc. Published by Sampson, Davenport & Company, 47 Congress Street, Boston, Mass.
(also same volume for the years 1872, 1874, 1878)

The Annual Statistics of Manufactures, Wright & Potter Printing Co., State Printers, 18 Post Office Square, Boston. ,
(multiple years 1886 – 1918)

*Seeger & Guernsey's Cyclopedia of Industry*_1890, 1901

Moody's Manual of Railroads and Corporation Securities, Twenty-Second Annual Number, Industrial Section, Vol II K-Z, 1921. Poor's Publishing Company, 33 Broadway, New York.

Maps & Atlases

Map of Hampden County, 1857, Henry F. Walling, Superintendent of the state Map, Boston.

Map of Hampden County 1870, Published by Beers, Ellis & Soule Co., New York, 1870

Atlas of Hampden County, 1894 L.J. Richards & Company, Springfield, Ma.

Atlas of Massachusetts, 1891 & 1904 Geo. H. Walker & Co., Boston, Ma.

Atlas of Westfield, 18884 – Geo. E. Walker & Sons, Boston, Mass

Census Records

    Federal Census Records   1830 – 1940

    Massachusetts Census Records 1855, 1865

Histories

History of Western Mass., the counties of Hampden, Hampshire, Franklin and Berkshire, Josiah Gilbert Holland, 1855, Published by Samuel Bowles and Company, Springfield, Ma.

History of Connecticut Valley, Louis H. Everts, J.B. Lippencott Co. Philadelphia, 1879

Westfield and it's Historic Influences 1669-1919, The life of an early town, Rev. John H. Lockwood, D.D. published 1922 by the author. Printing by Press of Springfield Printing and Bonding Co., Springfield, Ma.

Western Massachusetts History, Stephen Pitoniak, Jr., 1970, Self Published by author, Westfield, Ma.

Westfield Massachusetts 1669-1969, Edited by Edward C. Janes & Roscoe S. Scott, 1969, Westfield Tri-centennial Association, Westfield, Ma.

Experiences and Reminiscences of A Long and Busy Life, Frederick Morand, Westfield, Massachusetts, 1912

Mundale, The West Parish of Westfield, Massachusetts, Eloise Fowler Salmond

A Brief Historical Sketch of Wyben, Edward Caldwell Janes, 1935, unpublished.

Historical Essays of Windsor, Township & Village, Broome County, New York, Compiled and edited by Marjory Hinman, Pub. By to Town and Village Windsor, Broome County, New York, 1995